Treasures from the
Rijksmuseum
Amsterdam

Treasures from the
Rijksmuseum Amsterdam

Emile Meijer

Published in association with the Rijksmuseum Foundation

Scala/Philip Wilson

© 1985 Rijksmuseum, Amsterdam

First published in 1985 by Philip Wilson
Publishers Ltd and Summerfield Press Ltd,
Russell Chambers, Covent Garden, London WC2E 8AA

Translated from the Dutch by Annette Mills
Photography: G. Bijl (head photographer), P. Mookhoek, H. Bekker,
R. Taylor and K. Wesselius of the Rijksmuseum
Design: Rupert Kirby
Series editor: Kathy Elgin

Produced by Scala Istituto Fotografico Editoriale, Firenze
Phototypeset by Tradespools Ltd, Frome, Somerset
Printed in Italy

ISBN 0 85667 215 7 (UK)

ISBN 0.935748.63.6 (USA)
Library of Congress no. 84-052612

Front cover:
The merry drinker by Frans Hals

Back cover:
The meeting of the three kings by Adriaen van Wesel

Endpapers
One of the exhibition rooms of the museum in the 19th century, when it was housed in the
Trippenhuis. From a coloured wash drawing by Gerrit Lamberts.

Frontispiece
The main gallery of the Rijksmuseum, where Rembrandt's *The Night Watch* is displayed.

Contents

Dimensions

H = height
W = width
D = depth
Diam. = diameter

The following abbreviations, given in each caption, refer to the department of the Museum to which the object belongs.

PC = Paintings Collection
S&DA = Department of Sculpture and Decorative Arts
DH = Department of Dutch History
CAA = Collection of Asiatic Art
PR = Print Room

The Rijksmuseum seen across the canal.

Treasures from the
Rijksmuseum
Amsterdam

Foreword

The origins of the Rijksmuseum go back to 1798, the period of the Batavian Republic, when the property of the exiled Stadholder, Prince William V, was confiscated. Works of art which had been located in palaces all over the country were brought together in the Huis ten Bosch palace in The Hague, where a national museum was set up along French lines. This was known as the National Art Gallery and was opened to the public on 31 May 1800. The collection consisted of barely 200 paintings and a few objects of historical significance.

Today, nearly two hundred years later, this has expanded into a world-famous collection of approximately 5,000 paintings, 30,000 works of sculpture and the applied arts, 17,000 historical objects, 3,000 works of Asiatic art and a million prints and drawings. The collection is housed in the Rijksmuseum building on the Stadhouderskade in Amsterdam, which was begun in 1876 and opened to the public on 13 July 1885. The architect, Dr P.J.H. Cuypers, created a monumental building whose interior and exterior ornamentation recalled important personalities and events of national history and culture. Inside, however, there is practically nothing left of the original decor. Over the years the exhibition rooms have been constantly modernised, a process which has tended to remove the often superfluous decoration which many people felt distracted attention from the works of art.

The growth of the collection made repeated and rapid extension of the building necessary. Between 1898 and 1916 a new wing was built in two stages to house the modern art collection (the Hague School, works by Breitner), while after the second world war, when the collection of applied art grew with exceptional speed, three-storey constructions were erected in both inner courtyards to create considerable extra space for exhibition.

The Rijksmuseum owes its international reputation in the first place to the great Dutch painters of the seventeenth century, many of whose masterpieces are in its possession. Public interest, naturally, tends to focus on these works. However, the rest of the collection is equally impressive, as this book demonstrates. The selection of highlights illustrated here will provide an incentive to anyone reading the book to visit the museum and see the paintings and objects for themselves; for those who have already discovered the richness and variety of the collection, it will represent a confirmation of their personal experience.

S. H. Levie
Director

The meeting of the Magi
Adriaen van Wesel (*c*1420–Utrecht
*c*1490), 1475/77
*Oak, traces of polychrome; H. 76.5 cm, W.
91 cm*
From the Madonna Retable carved by the
sculptor Adriaen van Wesel of Utrecht
between 1475 and 1477 for the
Brotherhood of the Blessed Virgin in
's-Hertogenbosch and placed in their
chapel in the church of St John.   (S&DA)

Before 1500

The traditional image of the Netherlands – one of low-lying land and water – is reflected much less than one might expect in the visual arts. Nevertheless, Dutch art is considered to reach its highest point when its artists portray their country and fellow citizens. This occurred mainly in the first half of the seventeenth century, the latter part of the nineteenth and the beginning of the twentieth century, but the Rijksmuseum possesses at least one early example of art inspired by local circumstance. Because roughly half of the Netherlands lies below sea level, protected by dunes and dykes, flooding has always been a continual threat. The painting on p. 30/1 records a notable disaster of the fifteenth century, the St Elizabeth's Day Flood. This occurred during the night of 19 November 1421 and inundated a large area around the town of Dordrecht, leaving behind the present day marshy region of Biesbosch.

It is of course not only the nature of the Dutch landscape and geography that has determined the character of Dutch art over the centuries: political factors have also played a role, and in order to understand this properly, we must go back some thousand years. After the death of the Emperor Charlemagne in 814 AD, the Frankish empire, which stretched from the Rhine to the Mediterranean, was divided up among his three sons. The Netherlands were part of the middle portion, ruled by Lothair I, but by the tenth century had become part of the German Empire. The episcopal seat of Utrecht long dominated the earldoms and duchies which surrounded it but gradually the power of the German Emperor, who appointed and supported the bishop, waned and that of the counts of Holland became more dominant.

The earliest piece of Dutch sculpture in the Rijksmuseum dates from this period. This is a tympanum (p. 13) from the former abbey at Egmond, near Alkmaar, the oldest and most famous in the Netherlands, founded by the counts of Holland. It was an important mission centre, but was destroyed during the revolt against the Spaniards in 1572. The tympanum was originally above the main entrance of the abbey church and shows St Peter, flanked by Dirk VI, Count of Holland, and his mother Petronella. The Latin inscriptions read: 'O keeper of the Heavenly Gate, allow the faithful multitude kneeling before you to enter and be reconciled with the King of Heaven'. The inscription running horizontally reads: 'Here prays Dirk – this work was decorated by Petronella'. The tympanum was made between 1122 and 1132, probably by a monk from Egmond. The material is red sandstone and it originally served as a coffin lid, as shown by the grooves and dowels on the back in which rings could be fixed.

A remarkable object for use in church was the aquamanile, a vessel used for pouring water into the bowl in which the priest celebrating Mass would wash his hands. A variety of these medieval objects have survived, often taking the form of a lion, sometimes that of a knight on horseback, such as the bronze aquamanile from Hildesheim, Lower Saxony (p. 13). Relics of saints – either a part of their remains, often miniscule, or of their clothing – were much venerated in the Middle Ages and beautiful relic holders were made in order to emphasise the holiness of their contents. Elyas Scerpswert, a silversmith from Utrecht, made a relic holder for a church in the town in the form of a bust of St Frederick (p. 14). This is of partly gilded silver and dates from 1362, the period in which the Domtoren (Dom Tower) in Utrecht was built. Scerpswert's work shows the same exceptional qualities which characterise the work of Utrecht's silversmiths in later centuries.

Not all works of art were intended for the church, however; the aristocracy were also very fond of magnificent objects as an expression of their power and as a form of peaceful rivalry alongside the raw reality of political and dynastic conflict.

During a large part of the fourteenth century there was unrest in the Low Countries, both for domestic reasons and because of international political developments. The trade interests of the middle classes assumed ever-increasing importance and the growing wealth of the towns aroused the greed of the counts. Outside Holland, the eyes of the self-willed and powerful Dukes of Burgundy, members of the royal house of France, turned to the Dutch provinces. Philip the Good of Burgundy shrewdly exploited the differences between the various parties in Holland and Zeeland in order to add the two provinces to the territory which he already possessed, with the aim of reconstructing Lothair's Middle Empire. Because of his policy of centralisation, he can be considered the founder of the states of Belgium and Holland.

During their campaigns, the Dukes of Burgundy bivouacked in luxuriously decorated tents hung with tapestries designed by the foremost artists of the day (p. 14). These were easy to transport but were also used as permanent decoration in palaces, castles and public buildings. Similarly, there were small, portable paintings and statues which could be taken along when travelling, in addition to large wall paintings and statues for the adornment of buildings. The triptych in gold and enamel showing *Christ as the man of sorrows* (p. 14) is extremely small and is an example of a portable item which probably adorned the household altar of a member of the royal family or a noble. It was probably made in Paris around 1400.

Philip's son and successor, Charles the Bold, continued his father's policy, but died in 1477 without a male heir at Nancy while attempting to conquer Lotharingia (modern Lorraine) and thereby unite the Dutch provinces with Burgundy. His daughter Maria married the future Emperor Maximilian of Austria. The House of Burgundy thus gave way to that of the Hapsburgs and ultimately determined the future of the Netherlands, for it was under the Spanish branch of the Hapsburg family that the Dutch revolt against Spanish sovereignty was to begin.

While the Burgundian, Flemish and, to a lesser degree, the Dutch cultures were witnessing about this time the magnificent close of the Middle Ages, the birth of a new age was approaching in Italy. Politically speaking, the country was divided: the Popes were in conflict with the German Emperors but could not dispense with their support. The towns and their surrounding lands formed independent states, mostly controlled by a powerful family. The middle classes, in particular bankers and merchants, wanted more part in the running of the towns. This interplay of political and social powers left no-one untouched; the country was furthermore prey to disease, epidemics, storms and earthquakes. Nonetheless, the fine arts prospered, especially in Siena and Florence. The style was that of the late Middle Ages, although there was less interest in the Gothic than in France and Germany. The classical feeling for harmony had evidently survived the centuries, despite the fact that there was as yet no classical revival.

In painting, the emphasis fell on contours; the light was uniform and there was hardly any shadow. The subjects were mainly from the Old Testament and the Gospels, but there were also allegories on good and evil, righteousness and the vices. The cycle of human life and all its spiritual problems were probably more to the forefront in these turbulent times than in any other. Lorenzo Monaco, a painter who probably came from Siena and worked in Florence, where he died around 1425, painted a small panel showing St Jerome in his study (p.15), a subject which was very popular both at the time and long after for its representation of Faith, Charity, Power, Wisdom and Virtue within a limited space.

It was, however, in Flanders, the southern region of the Netherlands, that the great revolution in painting took place when the van Eyck brothers introduced the use of oil in paint. Introduce is perhaps not the word, since the use of oil as a binding agent in paint dates from earlier in the Middle Ages, but certainly Jan and Hubert van Eyck realised and exploited all the possibilities presented by the new medium. Paint to which oil has been added dries slowly, permits layers to be painted one over the other and makes it possible to add a layer of paint which has been mixed with a considerable amount of oil over an existing layer. This creates a layer of transparent colour, or glaze, which can be subtly shaded. Much more is known of Jan van Eyck than of the somewhat shadowy figure of his brother Hubert – it has even been doubted whether Hubert in fact existed. It was certainly Jan who painted the polyptych, showing the Lamb of God, in the Sint Baafskerk, Ghent, one of the greatest masterpieces of European painting.

Other famous painters of the first half of the fifteenth century included Hugo van der Goes, Rogier van der Weyden and Dirk Bouts. Bouts came originally from Oudewater in the North of the Netherlands, but moved to the South, probably because commissions were more plentiful there. During this period in the North there was as yet little in the way of art and culture and no great patrons of the arts to commission works. In the South, on the other hand, artists could benefit from the commissions for churches and monasteries and from private individuals, usually merchants from Flanders, Brabant and abroad. A well-known commission is that given by the Italian merchant Arnolfini to Jan van Eyck to paint his wedding portrait, a painting which is now in the National Gallery in London.

Sculpture, too, flourished during the first half of the fifteenth century in the South of the Netherlands and, unlike painting, remained of greater importance there than in the North. Wood carving was very common and many altarpieces were produced covered with carefully worked figures enacting Biblical events. The workshops in Antwerp and Brussels began to export carved wooden altarpieces in the fifteenth and sixteenth centuries and these travelled to all parts of Europe, even as far as the extreme north. A fine example of this type of work is the Southern Netherlandish altarpiece dating from about 1440 (p.15) which depicts *Christ's descent into limbo*, with the group of figures placed within a richly decorated frame. Remarkably, the original polychrome has largely been preserved and acts as a reminder of the close relationship between painting and sculpture.

More Northern Netherlandish wood sculpture has survived than stone, because wood carvings were easier to hide during the destruction of images by the Protestant iconoclasts in 1566, a period of great unrest which preceded drastic changes in the spiritual and political spheres in the North of the Netherlands. Wood was also more easy to obtain than stone, so it is likely that more wood carvings were produced. Whether or not this is indeed the case, the most renowned sculptor in the North during the last part of the fifteenth century was Adriaen van Wesel, who worked in wood. The group *The meeting of the Magi* (p.6) has all the characteristics of his work: the lively composition of the figures, the variation in each figure's attitude and character combined with a certain lack of sophistication in the characterisation. Because of the rich detail and landscape features which he incorporated, van Wesel is often termed a 'painter in wood'. The group probably formed part of a larger sculpture which has been lost, something which also applies to many of the other wood carvings of the period in the museum.

The artist whose real name is unknown but who is known as the Master of Koudewater, the place near 's-Hertogenbosch where his works originated, worked in a very different style. The carving of *St Barbara* (p16), with traces of polychrome, shows the saint standing quite literally on her father, who had her tortured and killed because of her conversion to Christianity. The Master of

Koudewater produced figures with very narrow waists, emphasised the folds of material in their garments and gave them a rather stiff bearing, which creates an air of gravity in his works.

Some impression of a noble tomb of the period can be gained from a bronze statue representing an unknown woman (p.17), once part of a series of ten adorning the tombstone of Isabelle de Bourbon in the former Abbey of St Michael in Antwerp. This is an example of the funeral cortèges, either carved or cast in bronze, which were placed around royal tombs, while the recumbent or kneeling figure of the deceased was surmounted on the tomb itself.

Geertgen tot Sint Jans, who worked in Haarlem, is considered to be the greatest painter in the North during this period. His work has much of the meditative atmosphere of the monastery. He lived in the house of the Sint Jan family as 'famulus et pictor' (servant and painter) as the inscription under an old engraving describes him. The painting in which Geertgen portrayed the *Holy Kinship* (Mary's family with St Anne as the central figure) is one of the most remarkable in Early Netherlandish painting (p.18). Of equal quality is another work of his, *The adoration of the Magi* (p.19), in which the ruins and landscape of the background are redolent of the atmosphere which Dutch painters knew so well how to create.

While Geertgen was painting his religious figures, meditating with his brush, as it were, on the bitterness and the sweetness of life on earth and on the solace which faith could provide, Piero di Cosimo in Florence was painting worldly portraits of the architect Giuliano da San Gallo and his father (p.21), relatively large against the background of the glorious Tuscan landscape. At the same time, another Italian artist, the Venetian Carlo Crivelli, was painting his *Mary Magdalene* (p.20), betraying in her mannered bearing and the sharply delineated folds of her dress the influence of the late Gothic style – he was, after all, thirty years older than Piero di Cosimo. But it was Cosimo's work which heralded in Italy the beginning of a new cultural era. The Renaissance marked the end of the Middle Ages and embodied characteristics which distinguished it conclusively from that period. The ideas which surfaced during the Renaissance were no longer primarily related to the spiritual life of man, his expectations with regard to life after death, and to heaven and hell, but were concerned with life on earth. This more worldly attitude considered man to be of central importance, a vision which was not only expressed in the arts but appeared in every facet of human activity.

The great artists of the Renaissance – Raphael, Michelangelo and Leonardo da Vinci – were masters of many forms of art. All three were architects as well as painters, while Michelangelo excelled as a sculptor and Leonardo had exceptional technical skills: Leonardo designed a statue of a horseman for Francesco Sforza of Milan and Michelangelo wrote poetry. Versatility was highly valued in the Renaissance: the *uomo universale*, the all-rounder, was seen as an ideal.

Architecture, sculpture, painting and the decorative arts all served many areas of social and religious life. Palaces arose side by side with churches next to town halls and houses for prosperous citizens. It is true that there had been much building, painting and sculpture at the height of the late Gothic era, especially in the wealthy territories ruled by the House of Burgundy, but in the Renaissance another new element was added to the newly acquired skills of perspective and anatomy – classical forms returned to architects' designs. Elements such as the pillar, capital, frieze and tympanum gave architecture a new look which many considered an improvement because of the prestige now attached to classical art. From about 1420 onwards these changes began to be consolidated in Italy.

At the height of the Renaissance came another world-shaking discovery – that of America by Columbus in 1492. The New World at once became the object of voyages made by men seeking to possess the riches which abounded there, but these were also voyages of conquest, since each nation naturally desired to monopolise the territories which offered such rewards. The Spaniards and Portuguese were the first, followed swiftly by the Dutch and the French. Immense riches did indeed emerge from the New World and they greatly altered the European economy. The change can perhaps best be described as an increase in scale: the average citizen probably noticed little improvement in his standard of living, but now there were larger palaces with larger parks around them, greater pomp amongst the nobility, richer bankers and more powerful merchants and, above all, a much greater military machine.

During this period Europe's political interest in Italy grew. Rome, Milan and Florence were, after all, the heart of the known world: in these cities lived the bankers who provided credit so that other countries could make war, and Rome was the seat of the head of the Catholic Church, who had great influence on world politics.

French military involvement in Italy in the late fifteenth century had important consequences for the arts. French officers, dazzled by the splendour they found there, bore the ideas and the styles of the Renaissance home to France, the most eminent among them rebuilding and designing their castles in those styles. It was in this period that the famous chateaux along the Loire came to full glory as the Renaissance took hold of cultural life in France. Under Francis I (1515–1647) Fontainebleau became the centre of a court modelled on those of the wealthy Italian princes and a meeting place for artists and craftsmen of all Europe.

Tympanum from the church of Egmond Abbey
Holland, *c* 1130
Variegated sandstone; H. 88 cm, W. 175 cm
Re-modelled from a coffin-lid, the tympanum shows Saint Peter,
Count Dirk VI of Holland and his mother, Countess
Petronella. (S&DA)

Aquamanile in the form of a knight on horseback
Hildesheim, Lower Saxony, 1st half 13th century
Bronze; H. 32 cm (S&DA)

13

Tapestry with the arms of Guillaume Roger de Beaufort (d. 1394) and Alienor de Comminges (d. 1397) [fragment]
Southern Netherlandish School(?), end 14th century (or later)
Wool; 220 × 210 cm   (S&DA)

Reliquary in the form of a bust of St Frederick
Elyas Scerpswert, Utrecht, 1362
Silver, partly gilded; H. 45 cm, W. 24 cm
Made for the Sint-Salvator (Holy Saviour)
Church, Utrecht.   (S&DA)

Household altarpiece (triptych)
Probably Paris, *c* 1400
*Gold and enamel; H. 12.7 cm, W. 12.5 cm
(open)*
The central portion shows Christ as the
Man of Sorrows, supported by an angel.
The inside of one wing shows the Virgin
and an angel bearing the Cross; the other
shows John the Evangelist and an angel
holding the lance and nails. The crest
shows the Coronation of the Virgin. From
Chocques Abbey.   (S&DA)

St Jerome in his study
Lorenzo Monaco (Siena (?) 1370/71 – Florence *c*1425), *c*1408
Panel; 23 × 18 cm   (PC)

Christ descending into limbo
Southern Netherlandish School, *c* 1440
*Oak with original polychrome and gilding; H. 48.5 cm, frame: H.
97.8 cm, W. 59.9 cm*   (S&DA)

St Barbara
Master of Koudewater (active in
's-Hertogenbosch *c*1460–70)
*Walnut with original polychrome; H.
92 cm*   (S&DA)

(below and right)
The annunciation
Tilman Riemenschneider (Heiligenstadt
c 1460 – Würzburg 1531), *c* 1480/85
Alabaster; H. 39 cm and 40.5 cm
                                (S&AA)

(following page left)
The Holy Kinship
Geertgen tot Sint Jans (Leyden (?) 1460/65 – Haarlem 1488/93), 1485
Panel; 137.5 × 105 cm (PC)

(following page right)
The adoration of the Magi
Geertgen tot Sint Jans (Leyden (?) 1460/65 – Haarlem 1488/93), c 1490
Panel; 90 × 70 cm (PC)

Statuette of unknown woman
South Brabant, 1476
Bronze; H. 58 cm
One of ten mourners from the tomb of Isabelle de Bourbon. (S&DA)

17

Mary Magdalene
Carlo Crivelli (Venice 1435/40 – Venice after 1493), 1485/90
Panel; 152 × 49 cm   (PC)

Giuliano da San Gallo
Piero di Cosimo (Florence 1462 – Florence 1521), *c* 1485
Panel; 47.5 × 33.5 cm (PC)

Francesco Giamberti
Piero di Cosimo (Florence 1462 – Florence 1521), *c* 1485
Panel; 47.5 × 33.5 cm (PC)

QVESTA·TAVOLA·A·FACTA·FARE
SVORA·CATERINA·FIGLIVOLA
DI·TOMASO·DI·SALVESTRO·DI
NVCCARELLO·ÑE·MCCCCC2

Retable with Madonna and Child between Saints Jerome and Nicholas of Myra
Benedetto Buglioni (Florence 1459/60 – Florence 1521), 1502
Majolica; H. 226 cm, W. 172 cm   (S&DA)

The Renaissance reached the countries of Western Europe rather late, around the middle of the sixteenth century, and bore clear traces of its mixed origin. Although there was direct contact with Italy, France was of course much closer. The movement which reached the Netherlands via Fontainebleau was a feature of the High Renaissance known as Mannerism: it was characterised by graceful, elongated forms and decorative elements derived from Roman art and featured motifs from the plant and animal world mingled with fabulous creatures, human heads, vases and candelabra, cleverly intertwined to constitute a new realm of shapes and forms. Another ornamental element introduced at the time was the cartouche, a frame round an image or a text whose dynamic form is thought to be derived from leather work.

An example of these motifs, known as 'grotesques', can be found as a decorative rim on a glazed earthenware dish from Castel Durante, Italy, made and decorated by Nicolò da Urbino (p.36). The scene in the middle of the dish is, however, of more importance than the rim. This is an allegorical representation of the calumny to which Apelles, renowned as court painter to Alexander the Great, nearly fell victim when he journeyed to Egypt after the death of his patron to work at Ptolemny's court.

An altarpiece (p.22) made of glazed terracotta and depicting the Virgin flanked by St Jerome and St Nicholas, gives some impression of the works being produced at this time in Renaissance Italy. The expressions of the figures are lifelike and, although modelled in relief, the figures are rounded and full. Their actions express emotion but they are at the same time dignified. The background contains a frieze, capitals, pilasters and an arch framing the enthroned figure of Mary – a perfect classical whole. Dated 1502, it is made according to the tradition of the workshop of Luca and Andrea Della Robbia and is attributed to a follower of theirs, Benedetto Buglioni.

The first of the sixteenth-century artists from the North of the Netherlands to travel to Italy was Jan van Scorel, born in a village near Alkmaar to the north of Amsterdam. It seems that his motive for travelling south was primarily a pious one. He travelled through Germany and Austria, embarked for Venice and finally landed at Jerusalem, the object of his pilgrimage. Hundreds of thousands of pilgrims had visited the Holy Land after the Crusades and the political situation there had made it possible. Scorel took advantage of his long pilgrimage to contact other artists, to learn from them and occasionally to execute a commission, as he did in Obervellach, Austria, where one of his triptychs still exists. After leaving Jerusalem he returned to Europe and to Rome, where Adrian VI, the only Dutch Pope in history, was at the time in office. Raphael, the favourite of the previous Pope Leo X, had died young in 1520, shortly before Scorel's arrival. Scorel must have regretted this if only for artistic reasons: his admiration for Raphael is clear from his *Mary Magdalene* (p.40). Scorel was appointed curator of the Belvedere collection in Rome, a post which Raphael had occupied. The marvellous papal collection of classical sculpture and architectural fragments taught Scorel much. This is evident from the changes his stay in Italy wrought in his work, which had previously been in the late Gothic mould. After his return to the North, he settled in the episcopal seat of Utrecht.

Scorel's pupil, Maerten van Heemskerck, who also came from the area to the north of Amsterdam, was no less influenced by classical Rome. Before his journey to Italy Heemskerck painted the sober, domestic portrait of a woman (p.41) which betrays his knowledge of the work of Jan van Scorel. Afterwards he recorded his visit to Rome in a series of sketches of the monuments of that city. He painted numerous works, some of them extremely large and all strongly influenced by Mannerism. Some were destroyed during the destruction of images by the iconoclasts.

Besides Jan van Scorel and Maerten van Heemskerck who are known to have travelled to Italy, there were other artists who stayed at home. Their real names are not always known and they are named after their works or the place where their most important works were found. The Master of Alkmaar, for example, whose real name was possibly Pieter Gerritsz, is named after seven panels, each representing one of the works of charity, which come from the Sint Laurenskerk (St Laurence's Church) in Alkmaar and date from 1504 (p.33–35). Another anonymous artist active during the same period is the Master of the Spes Nostra, named after the painting which portrays allegorically the vanity of human life (p.36). The work probably comes from the Augustinian monastery of Sion near Delft.

Two artists whose names are known are Jacob Cornelisz van

Oostsanen (or van Amsterdam) and Jan Mostaert, who was a pupil of Geertgen tot Sint Jans. Of the two, Jacob Cornelisz is most clearly a painter of the sixteenth century: Jan Mostaert's devout, somewhat doll-like style (p.36) recalls his master. The subject of Cornelisz' painting (p.40) is the incident from the Book of Samuel, where the disguised King Saul visits the Witch of Endor in her cave in order to consult the spirit of Samuel on how to remove the Philistine threat, since God no longer gives him counsel nor do his dreams advise him. Although Cornelisz' style is much livelier than that of Mostaert, both are clearly heirs of the Middle Ages, as is Jan Wellens de Cock of Flanders whose small triptych (p.32) shows Christ on the cross between the two thieves. The figures are elegant in form but somewhat meagre and insubstantial, recalling late medieval miniatures, an impression confirmed by the frame, which is ornamented in the late Gothic style.

During this period, art in the Netherlands was poised between the late Middle Ages and the new era. This becomes evident if one compares the embroidered hood from a cope dating from about 1520, which depicts the Dispute of St Catherine taking place in an interior which presents both late Gothic and Renaissance features (p.38), and a Brussels tapestry showing Christ washing Peter's feet (p.39), in which the attempt to achieve harmony of attitude and composition – especially in the presentation of the servant with the basin – is evidence of the acceptance of the Renaissance ideal. The persistence of Gothic forms well into the sixteenth century is illustrated once more, however, by the beautiful Northern Netherlandish dresser of about 1525 (p.38) which, in view of the emblems it bears, was probably the property of a guild of civic guards. The architectural structure of this oak dresser, with its diagonal columns and the tracery decorating the panels, is pure late Gothic.

Visitors to the Netherlands may notice, too, how the mid-sixteenth-century gable of the Gemeenlandshuis in Delft is still in the late Gothic style, whereas the old Raadhuis (Town Hall) in The Hague, built shortly after, is an example of the Renaissance style. There are, of course, a number of reasons why the adoption of a new style may be delayed: the desire to remain true to local tradition, a lack of architects or artists willing or able to work in the new style, or simply the question of materials. In the North of the Netherlands, for example, there was very little stone, the material in which Renaissance buildings were usually constructed, and importing it was expensive, so the use of wood persisted.

The sixteenth century is the century of the Reformation: Luther, Zwingli and Calvin in the field of religion and Erasmus in that of philosophy and humanism. The conflict arose in Switzerland and in Germany where, in 1517, Luther nailed his ninety-five theses to the door of Wittenberg Cathedral, in protest against the trade in indulgences, the belief in salvation through good works and the misuse of the sacrament of penance. At the same time Zwingli, a priest from Zürich, was preaching a new doctrine in Switzerland and later, Calvin brought reform to France. Social unrest, too, was a feature of the times. The first riots took place in Germany in 1524 and grew by the following year into a full-scale revolt by peasants in mid and southern Germany. Before the year was out, however, the revolt was bloodily suppressed and the established powers regained their authority.

It is against this background that one must consider the work of the German sculptor Tilman Riemenschneider of Würzburg and his contemporary Albrecht Dürer, the painter and engraver from Nuremberg. *The Annunciation* (p.16–17), a group consisting of two figures in alabaster, is an early work of 'Meister Til aus der Fransiskanergässe', as Riemenschneider was known. The Rijksmuseum also possesses a magnificent table ornament (p.44) of partly gilded silver and enamel made by Wenzel Jamnitzer, a goldsmith and engraver born in Vienna. It is three feet high and was made for the city council of Nuremberg, where Jamnitzer settled in 1534, the year in which he became a master of his guild. A contemporary and fellow townsman of Jamnitzer was Hans Sachs, the famous poet and mastersinger, known to music lovers from his role in Wagner's opera *Die Meistersinger von Nürnberg*. Another contemporary was Arent Coster of Amsterdam, to whom is attributed the horn of the Amsterdam Guild of Arquebusiers, made of buffalo horn and mounted in silver (p.42).

The Dutch counterpart of Albrecht Dürer was Lucas van Leyden, a child prodigy who, if one is to believe the oldest sources, was already engraving when he was nine and sold his first engraving when he was fourteen. Certainly van Leyden was engraving masterpieces, some of which are now in the Print Room of the Rijksmuseum, at a very early age and he also acquired renown as a painter when still very young. His famous triptych with *The Last Judgement*, which was commissioned by the van Swieten family as a *memento mori*, now hangs in De Lakenhal museum in Leiden. The Rijksmuseum possesses a number of his works, including a triptych depicting the Israelites dancing round the Golden Calf, a densely peopled scene which extends over the three panels (p. 42). Lucas had a colourful view both of Biblical events and of his own era, matched with an impeccable sureness of touch when depicting figures of various types in different attitudes. He was also a skilled still-life painter: eating and drinking utensils and food and drink are painted in minute detail, while the landscapes in the background provide evidence of his mastery of yet another field of painting. Several of his engravings portray the Dutch landscape in all its flat simplicity, revealing him as a forerunner of the seventeenth-century landscape painters.

The peasant boy in Pieter Aertsen's *The egg dance* (p. 46) is dancing not around the Golden Calf but around a number of eggs. The aim of this popular game was to dance round the eggs in clogs without breaking them. In this painting Aertsen portrays ordinary daily life, thus prefiguring the style of realism in painting which was to establish the reputation of the Netherlands in the seventeenth century.

Dutch painting is often compared to the Venetian because both express a refined feeling for colour and atmosphere. Nevertheless, the differences are more obvious than the similarities. Sixteenth-century Venetian paintings, in contrast to Dutch paintings, are large and monumental. The reasons for this lie not only in the temperament of the painters, but also in the greater wealth and broader vision of Venetian patrons. A renowned ensemble is the Villa Barbaro at Maser, designed by Antonio Palladio with frescos by Paolo Caliari, called Veronese. The building was commissioned by Daniele Barbaro, patriarch of Aquileia, and his brother Marcantonio. Daniele Barbaro was a scholarly and cultured man: his writings include a commentary on the architecture of Vitruvius, Augustus Caesar's architect, for which Palladio drew the maps, elevations and ornaments. Barbaro's portrait (p. 47), painted by Veronese, shows the published edition of this commentary and thus contains many elements of contemporary Venetian culture.

Another sixteenth-century Venetian painter, Jacopo Tintoretto, was like Veronese a painter of large, decorative canvases, many of which can be found in the Doge's Palace. Like Veronese, he was a superb portrait painter, as his *Ottavio Strada* (p. 49) proves. In 1581 Strada was appointed antiquarian to the court of Rudolf II, where shortly afterwards the Utrecht silversmith Paulus van Vianen was also to work.

Despite unrest, turbulence, rebellion, persecution, war and pillage, art and learning evidently flourished. There was a lively exchange between countries, and artists and scholars travelled quite freely in spite of obvious dangers. Death was an everyday affair and the dance of death was frequently portrayed in paintings. Life in this period, balanced between the Gothic and the Renaissance, between earth, heaven and hell, must have closely resembled the masterly infernal vision of Hieronymus Bosch.

In the second half of the century politics began to impinge on ordinary people's lives once more and it is in this period that the seeds of the Dutch revolt against the Spanish Hapsburgs were sown. The man who shaped the resistance to Spain and the new independent state was William I, Prince of Orange (1533–1584), known as William the Silent. The Rijksmuseum has his portrait painted around 1568 by Adriaen Thomasz Key (p. 50). The Dutch revolt was initially concerned with retaining the privileges granted by the Spanish king whilst opposing the centralised political system he championed. In addition, there was resistance to the introduction of permanent taxes by the governor, the Duke of Alva, sent to the Netherlands by Philip II to restore order and the authority of the Spanish crown after the 'iconoclastic fury' of 1566. By this point, religion had become a major factor in the revolt: the conflict between a legitimate government and its discontented subjects had become a struggle between Catholicism and Protestantism. In 1581 the northern provinces declared their independence. Three years later, Prince William was assassinated at the instigation of the Spanish king. But the battle was in effect over: despite their fluctuating fortunes, the northern provinces had won their independence, which was formally confirmed in 1648 by the Peace of Munster.

During this period the combat on land and at sea was so intense that one may well wonder how it was possible to pursue any other activity. If one considers trading activities and the achievements in painting, literature, music and scholarship, however, it would seem that the violence and warfare passed many people by.

By now, the flowering of the art of painting was heralding the advent of the seventeenth century: from this point onwards, Dutch painting began to free itself of international influence and approach the high point which it eventually reached in the sublime reproduction of everyday reality. This was a form of realism in which the 'ugly' became 'beautiful', a contradiction in terms which puzzled many a philosopher – how, they wondered, could a scene in a tavern with drunken peasants be beautiful? In order to answer the question they invented a new category of beauty, the 'picturesque', a term which is still used to describe the special nature of seventeenth-century Dutch painting.

The St Elizabeth's Day flood
Master of the St Elizabeth Panels (active late 15th–early 16th century), *c*1500
Panel; 127 × 110 cm
The panel is painted on both sides with scenes from the flood.　　　(DH)

30

31

Triptych: the scene on Calvary, with donors
Jan Wellens de Cock (active in Antwerp 1506–1527), *c* 1525
Panel; 37 × 25.5 cm (centre),
32.5 × 10 cm (wings)
When closed, the panels show St Christopher with the child Christ on the Way of Life. (PC)

The death of the Virgin
Master of the Amsterdam Death of the Virgin (active in northern Holland *c* 1500), *c* 1500
Panel; 58 × 78 cm (PC)

The seven works of charity
Master of Alkmaar (active in Alkmaar first
half 16th century), 1504
Panel; 101 × 54 cm (each panel)   (PC)

Feeding the hungry

Refreshing the thirsty

Clothing the naked

Burying the dead

Lodging the travellers

Visiting the sick

Comforting the captives

Dish with the calumny of Apelles
Nicolò da Urbino, Castel Durante (?), c1515/20
Majolica; Diam. 53 cm
On the rim are the arms of the Florentine Ridolfi family.   (S&DA)

The adoration of the Magi
Jan Mostaert (Haarlem c 1475 – Haarlem 1555/56), 1515/20
Panel; 49 × 35 cm   (PC)

Four Augustinian canons regular meditating beside an open grave
Master of the Spes Nostra (active in Delft or Gouda late 15th century), c 1505
Panel; 88 × 104.5 cm   (PC)

Triptych with the adoration of the Magi
Jacob Cornelisz van Oostsanen (Oostzaan before 1470 – Amsterdam 1533), 1517
Panel; 83 × 56 cm (centre panel), 83 × 25 cm (wings)   (PC)

Oak dresser
Northern Netherlandish School, *c*1525
Oak; H. 147 cm, W. 103.5 cm, D. 74.5 cm
From the Guild of Civil Guards in
Alkmaar. (S&DA)

**Hood from a cope with the dispute of
St Catherine**
North Netherlandish School (?), *c*1520
*Embroidered in silk with gold filigree on
linen, and small pearls; 53 × 49 cm* (S&DA)

(right)
Tapestry (detail)
Brussels, possibly from the workshop of
Pieter Pannemaker, *c*1520/25
*Linen, wool, silk and gold filigree;
300 × 315 cm*
The tapestry shows Christ washing
Peter's feet, Christ in the Garden of
Gethsemane, Christ being taken captive
and Christ before Caiphas. (S&DA)

Mary Magdalene
Jan van Scorel (Schoorl 1495–Utrecht
1562), *c* 1528
Panel; 67 × 76.5 cm (PC)

Saul and the Witch of Endor
Jacob Cornelisz van Oostsanen (Oostzaan
before 1470–Amsterdam 1533), 1526
Panel; 87.5 × 125 cm (PC)

Portrait of a woman
Maerten van Heemskerck (Heemskerk 1498–Haarlem 1574), *c* 1530
Panel; 84.5 × 65 cm (PC)

Triptych with the adoration of the golden calf
Lucas van Leyden (Leiden 1494–Leiden 1533) *c* 1530
Panel; 93 × 67 cm (centre panel),
91 × 30 cm (wings)   (PC)

Drinking horn of the Amsterdam Guild of Arquebusiers
Attributed to Arent Coster, Amsterdam, 1547
Buffalo horn and silver; H. 37.5 cm (S&DA)

Pompeius Occo (1483–1537)
Dirck Jacobsz (Amsterdam 1496–
Amsterdam 1567), *c* 1531
Panel; 66 × 54 cm   (PC)

Table ornament
Wenzel Jamnitzer (Vienna 1508–
Nuremberg 1585), 1549
*Silver, partly gilded, and enamel;
H. 99.8 cm*
Made for the Nuremberg city council.

(S&DA)

Tiled floor with the arms of the Montmorency family (detail)
Antwerp, 2nd quarter 16th century
Earthenware; 129.5 × 230.5 cm (entire floor)
Probably from one of the castles in France belonging to the family. (S&DA)

Allegory on the abdication of Emperor Charles V in Brussels, 25 October 1555
Frans Francken II (Antwerp 1581– Antwerp 1642), 1555
Panel; 134 × 172 cm (DH)

The egg dance
Pieter Aertsen (Amsterdam 1509–Amsterdam 1575), 1557
Panel; 84 × 172 cm   (PC)

Box, with the figure of Cleopatra and the arms of Bavaria
Probably Munich, 3rd quarter 16th century
Enamelled gold with diamonds and pearls; H. 10 cm, D. 5.6 cm
                                                              (S&DA)

Daniele Barbaro (1513–1570)
Paolo Veronese (Verona 1528–Venice 1588), *c* 1560
Canvas; 121 × 105.5 cm (PC)

Beggar's bowl and gourd
16th century
Wood and silver; Diam. 8 cm
The bowl and gourd were symbols of the
Geuzen (Beggars), who proudly accepted
the pejorative name 'beggars' given to
them by the Spanish.　　　　(DH)

Goblet with lid
Anno Knütgen, Siegburg, dated 1577
Earthenware; H. 31 cm
With the arms of Von Schwindt.

　　　　　　　　　　(S&DA)

Mortar
Attributed to Willem Wegewart the Elder,
Deventer, dated 1568
Bronze; H. 22.4 cm, Diam. 21.6 cm (S&DA)

Ottavio Strada (1549/50—1612)
Jacopo Tintoretto (Venice 1518–Venice 1594), 1567
Canvas; 128 × 101 cm   (PC)

49

Willem I (1533–1584), Prince of Orange
Adriaen Thomasz Key (Antwerp *c* 1544–Antwerp after 1589),
c 1568
Panel; 48 × 35 cm   (DH)

Woman from Oudendijk
Attributed to J. van Horst, 16th century
Oil on panel; 42 × 29 cm   (DH)

Woman at the spinning wheel and man with mug
Pieter Pietersz (Antwerp *c* 1543–Amsterdam 1603), *c* 1575
Panel; 76 × 63 cm   (PC)

Sir Thomas Gresham (1519–1579)
Anthonis Mor van Dashorst (Utrecht 1519–Antwerp 1575), *c* 1570
Panel; 90 × 75.5 cm   (PC)

Haarlem, Amsterdam and Utrecht all made an important contribution to the development of the arts at the end of the sixteenth and the beginning of the seventeenth centuries. In Haarlem, Cornelis Cornelisz was producing large-scale paintings such as *The fall of man* (p.52). Karel van Mander, who painted *The magnanimity of Scipio*, a story from classical history (p.68), was an extremely versatile artist and poet; his 'Schilder-Boeck' (Book of Painters), published for the first time in 1604, contains the biographies of most artists from classical times onwards and is still an important source of information concerning painters and painting in these earliest times. The patriarch of painting in the episcopal seat of Utrecht was Abraham Bloemaert who, throughout his long life (1564–1651), taught many painters who later became masters in their own right, including Hendrick ter Brugghen and Jan Both. He was himself a skilled painter, his work characterised by superb drawing and agreeable use of colour (p.68).

Many of the Utrecht painters born around 1580 travelled to Italy to complete their training or to seek commissions. Gerard van Honthorst lived there for some time and became known particularly for his candlelit scenes. *The merry fiddler* (p.76) is typical of his somewhat slick but faultless style of painting.

The Dutch painters who visited Italy became acquainted with the work of Caravaggio, an unconventional Roman painter whose unadorned realism caused great controversy at the time. His style of painting, particularly his dramatic use of chiaroscuro evidently had great influence on Dutch painters, especially those from Utrecht. One of the travellers to Italy was Hendrick ter Brugghen, Bloemaert's pupil. The influence of Caravaggio is evident in his work, in his *Adoration of the Magi* (p.74) and his portraits of Democritus, known as the laughing philosopher, and Heraclitus, the weeping philosopher (p.78). Still closer to Caravaggio in his use of sharply delineated outlines and light-dark contrast was another Utrecht painter, Dirck van Baburen. The representation of the burial of Christ which he painted for the San Pietro Church in Montorio became internationally famous through the engraving based on it. *Prometheus being chained by Vulcan*, a large canvas (p.77), is also typical of his work. Without Caravaggio and the Utrecht 'Caravaggistes', Rembrandt would probably never have used chiaroscuro in the way he did.

The fall of man
Cornelis Cornelisz van Haarlem
(Haarlem 1562–Haarlem
1638), 1592
Canvas; 273 × 220 cm   (PC)

53

Hendrick de Keyser also left his native town of Utrecht, but for Amsterdam rather than Italy, where he was appointed city mason – in modern terms, city architect. He was also a sculptor and created the monument to William the Silent which marks his grave in the Nieuwe Kerk in Delft. The terracotta bust of an unknown man (p.69) gives a good if somewhat limited idea of De Keyser's talent.

It seems that life in Haarlem, particularly at the beginning of the seventeenth century, had its cheerful side and this is often depicted in the paintings of the period. Both Esaias van de Velde and Dirck Hals, the younger brother of Frans Hals, painted joyous *fêtes champêtres* – outdoor parties (p.72 and p.76). William Buytewech moved in eminent circles, or at least received commissions from such quarters. His *Dignified couples courting* (p.73) shows two sisters choosing a husband: the elder sister holds out two rosebuds to the young man on the left in such a way that he has to take the one she wishes.

Frans Hals, the most famous of the Haarlem painters, was thus no exception to the rule with his occasionally very high-spirited scenes, such as the portrait *The merry drinker* (p.79), an officer who invitingly extends his full glass to us. Less exuberant but certainly far from gloomy is his wedding portrait of Isaac Massa and Beatrix van der Laen (p.75), an obviously well-to-do couple seated under a tree in their park. Frans Hals became known chiefly through his large group portraits of the civic guard, now in the Frans Hals Museum in Haarlem. The bravura brushwork, sparkling colour and the smiles and gestures of the figures are entirely characteristic of his style of painting.

The year 1600 did not of course represent a clear line of demarcation between the two centuries. Many artists who can be termed sixteenth-century painters continued their style of painting well into the seventeenth century. This is true of the landscape painter Joos de Momper of Antwerp. Born shortly after the middle of the sixteenth century, he remained active until 1635, painting beautiful mountain scenes with thrilling perspectives, cities on top of towering cliffs, reefs, bays full of ships and many other eventful scenes (p.70). All these landscapes, of course, had more to do with the imagination than reality – certainly none of them could be found in the Netherlands.

While de Momper was painting his bays, mountains and forests, however, other painters were more concerned with their own country, a land of polders, rivers and ditches. Hendrick Avercamp painted winter landscapes on Dutch canals (p.73) and Esaias van de Velde a ferry on a river in flat country surrounded by a mill, a church, farmhouses and trees – in short everything which is typical of the Dutch countryside (p.74). Since this was a new phenomenon in painting, there is a tendency to classify Joos de Momper and his fellows as relics of the previous century. *River Valley* (p.73) by Hercules Seghers, however, is also based on fantasy, or is at least imaginative in its composition, since each separate element is based on the study of nature. Seghers is mainly known for his colour etchings featuring a complicated experimental technique:

Rembrandt was a great admirer of Seghers and possessed a number of these etchings.

The arrival of the native landscape as a subject for painting in no way banished the imaginary – in fact the opposite is true, as we shall see. Alongside the simplicity of a bouquet of flowers in a glass, painted soberly but with love by Jan Brueghel the Elder (p. 70), fantasy reigned supreme in a number of spectacular works in silver. The brothers Adam and Paulus van Vianen brought a new form of decoration to silverwork, known as the 'Kwabornament' or Lobate Style, a fantastic interplay of flowing forms based on human anatomy. Their mastery of the human form as well as of landscape can be seen in the scenes they embossed on silver (p. 71, p. 75). The elder brother, Adam, worked in his native city of Utrecht until his death in 1627; Paulus died in middle age in Prague, where he was goldsmith at the court of the art-loving Hapsburg Emperor Rudolf II. The Amsterdam silversmith Johannes Lutma also used fantasy in both form and ornament (p. 83), while imaginative qualities and above all great plasticity are to be found in the bronze relief by Adriaen de Vries (p. 71). De Vries, born in The Hague and active in Florence, Rome, Augsburg and Prague, was sculptor to Rudolf's court. The Dutch appreciated the monumental rather more than may have been suggested. Both the work of Adriaen de Vries and the fragment of a Delft tapestry showing a mythological scene (p. 69) are proof that there was definitely considerable appreciation for large-scale ornament; the problem was that artists needed patrons who were willing to commission such works. Dutch patrons, mainly merchants, were rarely prepared to do so.

During the same period that Frans and Dirck Hals were painting merry portraits of their fellow-citizens and Ter Brugghen and the other Utrecht painters were developing the use of chiaroscuro in portraits of ordinary people as characters from the Bible and antiquity, the young Rembrandt van Rijn was developing his own art in Leiden. Born the son of a prosperous miller in 1606, he was soon apprenticed to a now virtually forgotten Leiden painter, van Swanenburgh. Later, however, he studied for a few months under Pieter Lastman of Amsterdam, a painter whose varied subjects and supple, academic style are gaining greater appreciation among modern art historians. Lastman had visited Italy: Rembrandt himself would never go there because, he said, he had too little time. He nevertheless studied the work of the Italians extremely closely, at Lastman's studio, at auctions and in private collections.

Rembrandt returned to Leiden for several years, during which period his fame began to grow, according to a contemporary – who added, however, that the fame was probably premature. This writer, a lawyer from Utrecht, noted that Rembrandt excelled in the portrayal of human passion. His paintings from this period are mainly small and extremely carefully worked. His deeply shadowed *Self portrait* of 1628 (p. 78) dates from this period, as does *Tobias accusing Anna of stealing the kid* (p. 77). The contrast between light and shade was already important, except in his very earliest works.

From the beginning he painted numerous self portraits and portraits of people around him: in Leiden this included his parents, his family and faces seen in the street. It is thought that the old woman who appears several times in his portraits, once as the prophetess Anna (p.80), was his mother. This woman was also painted (p.80) by Rembrandt's first pupil, Gerard Dou. Dou, in his day, was widely renowned for his deceptively lifelike portrayal of ordinary people and everyday objects, and he continued to work in virtually the same style and small format throughout his career. A Leiden school grew up consisting of followers of Gerard Dou, the most famous and the most talented of them being Gabriel Metsu (p.100). These 'fine painters' continued to work in this style until well into the eighteenth century.

In the course of the seventeenth century Leiden developed into one of the most important textile manufacturing towns in Europe. It was, however, outstripped by Amsterdam and it was doubtless the temptation of more and greater commissions that lured Rembrandt to the trading city on the IJ in 1631, a move which was to become permanent. From Rembrandt's first ten years in Amsterdam, the Rijksmuseum possesses a portrait of Maria Trip (p.83), a distinguished member of the urban patriciate who built their stately houses on the canals and embankments of the city. Rembrandt himself spent his most successful period in a substantial house on the Jodenbreestraat with his wife Saskia van Uijlenburch, daughter of the burgomaster of Leeuwarden, and after her death with Hendrickje Stoffels. Both women feature in numerous portraits.

Rembrandt completed the painting whose full title is *The company of Captain Frans Banning Cocq and Lieutenant Willem van Rutenburch,* but which is universally known as *The Night Watch,* in 1642 (p.84). Although it is a group portrait, it is distinguished by the lively treatment of the figures, the dashing way in which they move and above all by the beautiful glow produced by the uniforms. While he was living on the Jodenbreestraat Rembrandt painted *The anatomy lesson of Dr Joan Deyman* (p.94), a large section of which was unfortunately lost in a fire in 1723.

In 1656 Rembrandt was in serious financial difficulties, as were many Dutchmen after Holland's defeat in the war at sea against England. He was finally forced to sell his house and art collection and in 1660 he moved to a house on the Rozengracht where he spent the last years of his life, not far from the symbol of Amsterdam, the Westerkerk with its unique tower. He probably painted *St Peter's denial* (p.97) in the house on the Rozengracht, where he was extremely active. In total contrast to the picture generally held of the old, ignored and poverty-stricken Rembrandt of this period he appears, in fact, to have been full of energy. In 1660 he portrayed his son Titus in a monk's habit (p.97) and in 1661 he painted *The Syndics* (p.98). The Syndics were the officials who were responsible for supervising the quality of the cloth manufactured by the members of the Amsterdam drapers' guild. The 1661

Self portrait as the Apostle Paul (p.97) may well show a shockingly aged man compared to the earlier self portraits, yet his productivity during this time would appear to deny that this was so.

The painting known as *The Jewish bride* (p.103), for which Vincent van Gogh had boundless admiration doubtless both for the fervour it expresses and for its glowing colour, dates from around 1667. The picture probably portrays a Jewish couple, the poet Don Miguel de Barrios and his wife Abigaël de Pina, portrayed as Isaac and Rebecca in Isaac's tent. Many other suggestions have also been made about the nature of this painting – some hold it to be merely a double portrait, others another scene from the Bible.

Rembrandt was also skilled in drawing and etching and it is in these works that his feeling for the Amsterdam of the period is expressed. He drew and etched scenes around Amsterdam, in small villages, along rivers and in polders; along the Amstel and the Vecht, in Diemen, Amstelveen, Halfweg and to the north of the city in Durgerdam, Buiksloot and Landsmeer – works that reveal all the beauty of the Dutch countryside. In the city itself he drew and etched the Amstel where it flows through the city along the Rokin into the IJ. He drew ships on the IJ, and the streets and bridges of the city. But he did not only draw the gables and streets, he also portrayed the inhabitants – strollers, merchants, beggars, peasants and orientals, gentlemen and servants.

Rembrandt lived during the height of Amsterdam's prosperity. Trading companies were established there which did profitable business with Indonesia, America, Africa, China, Japan, the Baltic, Northern Russia, England, France, Spain, Portugal and the Levant. Banking flourished as a result of the need for credit guarantees and investment capital for international trade. Shipbuilding expanded to meet the growing need for ships for the merchant fleet and the navy, which had to protect trading vessels as well as wage war against the enemy. The ship-building industry required wood and in 1606 the first saw-mill went into operation: 50 years later there were between 50 and 60 such mills in Amsterdam. The increase in trade and industry was accompanied by a rise in the population as people came to the city from other parts of the Netherlands. In 1585 the city had no more than 30,000 inhabitants; in 1630, at the time of Rembrandt's removal there from Leiden, it had about 115,000 and in 1675 over 200,000.

Rembrandt was only the most famous of many notable painters who lived and worked in seventeenth-century Amsterdam. He had numerous pupils, the best of whom developed their own style, although it was impossible to disguise the influence of their teacher. Govert Flinck's conception of painting, for instance, is very close to that of Rembrandt: nevertheless, *Isaac blessing Jacob* (p.81), painted in 1638, has something original in its composition (the half figures) and in its use of colour. The same is true of a later pupil, Nicolaes Maes, whose *Old woman in prayer* (p.93), painted around 1655, is one of the most popular paintings in the Rijksmuseum. It is remarkable for its technical skill and the poetic feeling with which Maes has painted this intimate moment of saying grace. Maes portrayed another kind of reflection in *The daydreamer* (p.93), a Rembrandtesque portrait of a girl in a window entwined with branches bearing peaches. The colour of the opened shutter is the key to the whole composition.

Cultural life in Amsterdam was of course not only a question of painting. There were many writers, actors, sculptors, musicians and scholars, some of them brilliant and many of them closely connected, either through family relationships or through mutual interest and attraction. Two members of the urban patriciate with literary talent were P.C. Hooft and Roemer Visscher. Visscher had two talented daughters, Anna Roemers and Maria Tesselschade, one of whose many skills was engraving on glass: the rummer on page 74 was engraved by Anna Roemers. Another member of their circle was the renowned organist and composer Jan Pieterz Sweelinck, who gave recitals in the Oude Kerk which were open to the public.

Rembrandt, too, had many well-placed connections, not the least being his wife Saskia van Uijlenburch and her distinguished Frisian family. In addition, though, there were his countless pupils and their circles of acquaintances, and the dozens of people whose portraits he painted, etched or drew. He corresponded with Huygens concerning commissions, collected works of art, visited galleries and auctions, lived in his own substantial house with all the responsibilities this involved, and created an œuvre which is so immense that it is surprising he ever found time for other activities and relationships. It is difficult to say which of Rembrandt's relationships were business contacts and which of them were personal. How friendly, for example, was his relationship with the Jewish scholar and printer Menasse ben Israel, who lived opposite him in the Jodenbreestraat? Rembrandt etched ben Israel's portrait and illustrated one of his books. He also knew Dr Franciscus van den Ende, an extremely stimulating personality whose fascinating life story has only recently been published. Van den Ende was the teacher of the philosopher Spinoza, a poet, diplomat, art dealer, producer of plays and finally a conspirator against Louis XIV.

Cultural life during the Republic was not of course limited to Amsterdam, but Amsterdam was by far the most important town and set the pace culturally, politically and economically. Anyone wishing to see the power of Amsterdam depicted in marble and stone should visit the Town Hall – now a Royal Palace – on the Dam, or see it portrayed in paintings and prints. The Town Hall, as already noted, was intended to commemorate the 1648 Peace of Munster, in which the Republic was recognised as an independent power. The United Netherlands, however, were not always of one mind. The common struggle against Spain was constantly hampered by domestic political and religious differences whose fundamental cause was often far from clear.

Although there are prints and poems dating from this period and the odd painting which offers a biting commentary on contemporary events, these are mostly in allegorical form and no such observations can be found in the masterpieces which established the reputation of seventeenth-century Dutch painting. Perhaps that is precisely their attraction: that with artistic licence they portray the country, the people, their towns, houses and living rooms as though life were never disturbed by war, revolution, disease or death. A painting such as *The sick child* by Gabriel Metsu (p.100) moves us because it is exceptional in showing the illness of a child as an object of domestic concern and personal anxiety.

The great admiration which Dutch landscape painting has attracted through the centuries is inspired by its capacity to capture nature in all its moods – or, rather, the mood experienced by man when he surveys the countryside. The first painter to reproduce, rather than merely reflect, the intimate majesty of the Dutch landscape was Jan van Goyen, a pupil of Esaias van de Velde, who painted *Landscape with two oaks* (p.85). Van Goyen painted open vistas; river banks with willows and other trees, enlivened with farmhouses, steeples profiled against the distance and peasants, mostly idle rather than at work. He was a painter who worked rapidly in a loose, dashing style like some of the Impressionists and had none of the stately precision of Jacob van Ruisdael, the great landscape painter of the following generation. Van Goyen's colours were based on grey, with greenish or bluish tones and here and there a brighter touch.

Salomon van Ruysdael, Jacob van Ruisdael's uncle, was about ten years younger than van Goyen and also excelled in the painting of willows along the riverside – he could convey the trembling of the leaves in the light better than any other painter. However, to admire him simply for that would be to do him a great injustice. His portrayal of clouds driven through the sky, the subtly-shaded reflections of light in water, and the microscopic precision with which he painted treebark and cowhide within the broader context of the landscape, win him a special place in Dutch landscape painting (p.88).

Paulus Potter, a generation younger than van Goyen and Salomon van Ruysdael, is the most famous painter of animals of the seventeenth century. His reputation was established by the life-size painting of a young bull, which he painted with the same precision as Gerard Dou would paint a broomhandle or an earring. However, most of his devotees prefer his smaller paintings since they better express the sobriety of the landscape and the character of the cattle and horses within it (p.88). To paint animals as if one were making a portrait was new at the time, but few would now call Paulus Potter a revolutionary.

Winter landscapes had, by contrast, long been accepted as a subject. The works of Aert van der Neer, however, show how a traditional subject can constantly give rise to new interpretations (p.89). A pale light shining from a lofty sky with motionless clouds illuminates small figures on an endless frozen waterway. There is nonetheless a trace of warmth, as if the winter sun was about to break through. Van der Neer produced superb light effects and was mainly known for his landscapes by moonlight.

Everyday reality, one might think, offers painters an inexhaustible variety of subjects. Yet seventeenth-century painting revolved around a limited number of themes, albeit with numerous variations. Furthermore, many painters specialised in only one or two subjects. Landscapes under poetic moonlight were, as has been seen, the speciality of Aert van der Neer; Adriaen and Isaack van Ostade painted scenes in taverns and farmhouses. The elder brother, Adriaen, was a pupil of Frans Hals and in his turn taught Isaack. Adriaen's picture of skaters in a farmhouse (p.89) gives a very disorderly and therefore very realistic impression – one has only to look at the individual objects and figures to realise that this somewhat shabby gathering in a Rembrandtesque half-darkness is painted with wit and precision and with the most subtle colour shading.

It seems that around the middle of the seventeenth century and for ten to fifteen years afterwards, more paintings were produced which gave an effect of stillness and quiet than in the rest of the century put together. Even a moment of booming noise, when the home fleet fired its guns in salute on approaching the state barge with Prince Frederick Henry on board was portrayed by Jan van de Capelle as a reflection in tranquil water (p.90). A rather more conventional theme for reflection in water is the winter landscape, and van de Capelle created such landscape paintings full of atmosphere. The view under the bridge (p.91), where heaven and earth meet in miniature, reveals the care with which the painter chose his viewpoint, and we may therefore conclude that other details such as the proximity of the frosty treetops to each other and the white crested clouds were also the result of meticulous care. Jan van de Capelle was a wealthy man: he ran a family cloth-dyeing business, was a possessor of property and a yacht (which he probably used as a 'floating studio') and owned one of the largest art collections of the time, including paintings and drawings by the seascape painters Simon de Vlieger and Jan Porcellis, and by Jan van Goyen, Rembrandt, Rubens, Hals, van Dyck, Brouwer, Hercules Seghers and Avercamp. The number of drawings he possessed is remarkable: over 500 by Rembrandt, more than 400 by Jan van Goyen and about 1,300 by Simon de Vlieger.

The silence breathed by Pieter Saenredam's *Interior of St Odolphus church in Assendelft* (p.88) derives from the harmonious lines of the architecture, the pale colours and the geometric construction, which gives a heightened sense of perspective. The church itself is definitely not silent: the minister is standing in the pulpit and ministers do not whisper but fill the space with their exhortations and prayers as the congregation sing God's praises. In the foreground is the tombstone of Saenredam's own father; the stone on the right marks the family grave of the lords of Assendelft in the province of North Holland where the painter was born in 1597. Pieter Saenredam specialised in the drawing and painting of architecture, mainly that of churches, and is distinguished by his meticulous accuracy. In many of his paintings he notes the measurements of the building in question. Paintings by Saenredam are, in fact, a source of reliable information when churches are restored, although he permitted himself a degree of artistic licence where colour was concerned. He worked mainly in Haarlem, but also in 's-Hertogenbosch, Assendelft, Alkmaar, Utrecht, Amsterdam and Rhenen.

Another architectural painter of the same generation as Saenredam was Gerrit Houckgeest, who worked principally in Delft, where he painted the interiors of the Oude and the Nieuwe Kerk (Old Church and New Church) (p.92). Unlike Saenredam, he chose oblique perspectives through the church, often with part of the building in the foregound, thereby creating a very spacious effect. His light effects are also more varied than those of Saenredam. He allows more light to enter his churches – sometimes even the rays of the sun – and introduces everyday life in the form of men, women and children who stroll around, chat to each other, observe and play; occasionally there is even a dog.

The fact that paintings with an animal as principal character were not purely the province of Paulus Potter is shown by the large canvas showing an angry swan defending its nest against a dog swimming in the water. However, while Potter made animals the subject of his entire œuvre, Jan Asselijn, the painter of *The threatened swan* (p.90), mainly painted Italian landscapes. The swan was later turned into a political allegory by the addition of a number of inscriptions to the painting: it represents the vigilance of Johan de Witt, the Grand Pensionary (the swan), defending Holland (the nest) against the enemies of the state (the dog). Whether it is an allegory or simply a scene from nature, it is a masterly painting, pervaded by a warm light which emphasises the beauty of the bird in an imposing fashion.

Jan Asselijn lived in Italy from 1635 to 1646 and became one of the group known as the 'Italianates' – Dutch landscape painters who settled in Italy for long or short periods and painted the Italian landscape in a style which was unknown in Italy. With a typically Dutch feeling for the picturesque, they painted Roman streets with beggars, hawkers and artisans. This genre was developed by Pieter van Laer in particular, and he had many followers. The principal subjects, however, were landscapes with figures, mostly herdsmen with their cattle, occasionally depicting a Biblical or mythological scene, and riverscapes, often with waterfalls and ruins. What was special about the work of the Italianates was the golden light which they rendered in such a masterly way and which constitutes the great charm of their landscapes. The greatest exponent of this genre – indeed one may call him the originator – was Jan Both of Utrecht, a pupil of Abraham Bloemaert. It is hard to believe that when Jan Both painted the landscape shown here (p.91), he had been back in Utrecht for nearly ten years. He cut short his stay in Italy after the unfortunate death of his brother Andries, who was drowned in a canal in Venice.

Aelbert Cuyp of Dordrecht was an 'Italianate' who stayed at home, painting Italy's golden light from his imagination and, of course, from the works of his contemporaries who had been there.

His *River landscape with riders* (p.93) is half fantasy, half reality. The scene would seem to be located on the river Rhine, either in Holland or in Germany, near Wageningen or Kleef. However, any desire to know exactly what location inspired Cuyp's painting disappears as soon as one becomes absorbed in its warm light.

Jan Both had great influence on the other Italianates, including Adam Pijnacker. He, too, remained in Italy for only a short period of three years, yet his work includes some of the most original in the Italianate genre, both daring and lively. His rendering of an everyday scene on the shore of an Italian lake, where a barge is being unloaded (p.102) is remarkable for its extremely realistic yet unusual composition. Visitors to the Museum will have noticed that such an everyday scene as this was rarely painted by artists 'at home', perhaps because it would have been considered too ordinary. Another explanation, of course, might be the more obvious one, that life in Italy tends to be lived outdoors, whereas in cold and windy Holland people spend much of their time indoors.

The paintings of Jan Steen would appear to corroborate this theory: his scenes are from everyday life, but always indoors. Steen is renowned for his 'households' – interiors with large families gathered together for amusement or at table. The mood is usually fairly frivolous and indeed the term 'a Jan Steen household' is to this day applied to a lively and untidy home. Sir Joshua Reynolds, the eighteenth-century portrait painter who was President of the Royal Academy and gave an annual address to the students on art in general and painting in particular (the 'Discourses on Art'), described Steen thus: '... if this extraordinary man had had the good fortune to be born in Italy, instead of in Holland, had he lived in Rome instead of Leiden, and been blessed with Michelangelo and Raphael for his masters instead of Brouwer and van Goyen; the same sagacity and penetration which distinguished so accurately the different characters and expression in his vulgar figures would, when exerted in the selection and imitation of what was great and elevated in nature, have been equally successful; and he now would have ranged with the great pillars and supporters of our Art.'

Sir Joshua Reynolds' opinion of Steen is not nowadays widely shared; few people are offended, as he was, by the vulgarity of Jan Steen's subjects. Indeed, it will be clear to anyone who looks carefully at his pictures that these are not random moments but are carefully staged. *The sick woman* for example (p.100), creates the impression of a performance rather than of an eye-witness account of a real doctor's call. It is nowadays assumed that paintings such as this – for the theme does occur elsewhere – are an allusion to disappointed love, an affliction of the spirit which was in those days considered to be a physical ailment. Furthermore, the coat the doctor is wearing as a symbol of his status had been abandoned by the profession long before the seventeenth century: doctors were by then only dressed in this way on stage. It has therefore been concluded that paintings depicting doctors' calls were also satires on those doctors who shamed their profession: the charlatans,

62

swindlers and money-grubbers.

Another theme which Steen used more than once was a Dutch proverb which translated runs: 'The young ones chirrup as the old ones used to sing', meaning that the young tend to imitate their elders. He gives a literal representation of this (p.103) in the form of a family party with the older people singing and a young boy playing the flute, although the bagpipe player in the corner by the window (a self portrait) has already left his youth behind and his chirruping does not therefore correspond exactly to the meaning of the proverb.

Steen's *The feast of St Nicholas* (p.96) is enormously popular, not only because of its qualities as a work of art, but because St Nicholas' Day (5 December) is still celebrated in the Netherlands and the subject is therefore one of general interest. The didactic intention of the painting is illustrated by the weeping boy on the left: he has been naughty, and St Nicholas has not brought him a present.

Sir Joshua Reynolds was at least correct when he praised Steen for his characterisation, for whether one sees a hidden meaning in his paintings or not, his figures never leave us in doubt as to their character or role. When Steen paints small, intimate scenes such as *Woman at her toilet* (p.96), the obscure allusions are lost to modern viewers and they concentrate instead on the fine drawing, the subtle colour-shading and the warm light in which Steen has bathed the bedside.

Interiors were also a favourite subject of an older colleague of Steen's, Gerard ter Borch of Zwolle, who travelled widely and was mainly active in Deventer. His group in an interior (p.92) was once called *The paternal admonition* until it was noticed that during this *Gallant conversation*, as the painting is now known, the officer on the right is raising his right hand not in exhortation but to show a shining coin to the young lady. Ter Borch painted numerous portraits, virtually all of them small in size. Dressed in all her finery, little Helena van der Schalcke (p.86) looks more like a small princess than the daughter of a North Holland preacher that she was.

Genuine royalty was painted by Bartholomeus van der Helst when he made the portrait of Princess Henrietta Maria Stuart, widow of Prince William II and mother of King and Stadholder William III (p.92). The satin dress, painted brilliantly by van der Helst who was a master of such detail, and the silver armchair lend a royal splendour to the portrait, but the attempt to convey the royal manner was a failure.

The death of William II in 1650 marked the beginning of what is known as the first stadholderless period, which was to last until 1672. During this period, the Netherlands fought two naval wars with England and one with Sweden. All three were trade wars. However, the second war with England (1665–1667) also involved dynastic interests: Charles II, on the throne since the fall of Cromwell in 1660, was working for the return of his nephew, the future William III, as stadholder. The most spectacular battle between the two fleets was the Four Days' Battle from 11–14 June 1666, when the Dutch fleet under the famous admiral Michiel Adriaansz de Ruyter defeated the English under George Monk and Prince Robert of the Palatine. Throughout the battle an artist moved between the fighting ships in a galiot (a type of ketch) which had been put at his disposal, observing the struggle from the most advantageous position and making innumerable sketches. The artist was Willem van de Velde of Leiden, known as the Elder, since his son was also a painter. He used an unusual technique that makes his paintings stand out in any collection: he drew with pen and ink on carefully prepared white linen. The fine point of the pen enabled him to reproduce the smallest detail with perfect clarity (p. 102).

Van de Velde was often accompanied by his son when he set off to make one of his pictorial reports of an action at sea. With the exception of the innumerable sketches which served as study material, the latter produced virtually only paintings. It is both painters' feeling for the moods of the sea, which they rendered in such a masterly way (p. 118), and their ability to combine artistic talent with a comprehensive technical knowledge of shipping and sea warfare that make the van de Veldes great painters. When the 1672 war broke out, they left the Republic and settled in England, where they became painters at the court of Charles II, the great enemy of Johan de Witt. This did not prevent the city of Amsterdam from giving the younger van de Velde (who was then over fifty) a commission to paint the harbour of Amsterdam during a brief visit to the city in 1686.

The landscape painter Jacob van Ruisdael lived for a time in Amsterdam. His house was near the Dam and a number of paintings have been preserved showing his view over the square. However, the most important work from his Amsterdam period is the view of the *Windmill at Wijk bij Duurstede*, one of the most popular paintings in the Rijksmuseum (p. 111). For those who know Holland as the country of windmills, it is interesting to note that landscape paintings showing windmills are relatively rare in the seventeenth century: the image of the windmill as a typical feature of the Dutch landscape only came into existence in the nineteenth century. Perhaps this is one of the reasons for the unusual popularity of Ruisdael's mill. It is an exceptional painting in which the mill is portrayed in its most expressive form, as a mighty shape rising up against a melancholy, cloudy Dutch sky. The broad, reflecting expanse of the river is, of course, the epitome of Holland at its most beautiful. Ruisdael, generally deemed to be the greatest Dutch landscape painter of the seventeenth century, could build up landscapes on a grandiose scale without forgetting detail. No-one could paint the characteristic features of different trees or the dune vegetation around Haarlem as well as he. The view of Haarlem that Ruisdael observed from the dunes of Overveen, which lies between Haarlem and the sea, is not only an impressive portrait of the town amidst broad, flat countryside, but also a picture of seventeenth-century industry. Seen in sloping perspective, the bleaching fields between the dunes and the city – which was supplied with clean dune water – were an essential element in the process of linen manufacture.

Both Ruisdael and Johannes Vermeer of Delft must be included among the three or four greatest painters of the seventeenth century. Vermeer's œuvre is relatively small, consisting only of about thirty paintings. One may therefore conclude that he worked slowly or with long intervals between paintings. The first explanation is probably the most accurate, for anyone who studies the four paintings in the Rijksmuseum (p. 95, p. 98 and p. 101) will be struck by the meticulous attention to detail, which must have demanded a great deal of time. But however worthy of admiration this precision is, it must not be forgotten that it is only a technical means which he employed to create an extraordinary combination of subject matter, colour and light. His subjects were as simple as could be imagined: a few houses, a woman pouring milk, a woman receiving a letter, a woman reading a letter.

Pieter de Hooch, a Rotterdammer by birth, also lived in Delft and painted interiors. His works have been compared with those of Vermeer, but are less focused on a single motif and frequently incorporate a view through an open doorway or an arch to deepen the perspective (p. 99).

Delft is also the home of the famous pottery, which in form and colour was inspired by costly, imported Chinese porcelain and was originally sold as a cheaper but similar type of product (p. 89). In the seventeenth and eighteenth centuries there were numerous pottery factories in Delft and in other places in the Republic. Although blue Delft is the most famous, multicoloured glazed pottery was also made and white Delft was also a speciality. A special line of production was the manufacture of tiles which were decorated with patterns or scenes and which were sometimes fitted together to form a panel or picture (p. 117). These were intended as wall coverings, for instance, or for the back wall of a fireplace.

Plane with attached plane-iron
Netherlands, end of 16th century
Beechwood; 16.8 × 6.3 × 10.9 cm, Iron, 13.8 × 4 cm
These were among the carpentry tools taken on Willem Barents'
expedition (1596–1597) and used during the winter spent on Nova
Zembla. (DH)

**Bust of Pope Gregory XIV (1590–
1591)**
Bastiano Torrigiani (Bologna?–Rome
1596), 1590/91
Bronze; H. 31 cm (S&DA)

Copper kettle
Netherlands, end of 16th century
Copper; H. 22 cm, Diam. 33 cm
This was among the cooking utensils
taken on Willem Barents' expedition
(1596–1597) and used during the winter
spent on Nova Zembla. (DH)

Pendant with wedding symbols
South Germany, second half 16th century
Gold, enamel and precious stones;
H. 10 cm, W. 6 cm   (S&DA)

Double goblet
Hans Petzolt (1551–1633), Nuremburg,
end 16th century
Gilded silver; H. 54 cm   (S&DA)

67

The magnanimity of Scipio
Karel van Mander (Meulebeeke 1548–
Amsterdam 1606), 1600
Copper; 44 × 79 cm   (PC)

The preaching of John the Baptist
Abraham Bloemaert (Gorinchem 1564–
Utrecht 1651), *c* 1600
Canvas; 139 × 188 cm   (PC)

**Prince Maurits at the Battle of
Nieuwpoort**
Pauwels van Hillegaert (Amsterdam
1595–Amsterdam 1640), 1600
Panel; 82.5 × 117.5 cm   (PC)

Tapestry with Procris taking leave of Diana (detail)
Delft, workshop of Frans Spierings, signed, *c* 1610
Wool and silk; 345 × 520 cm   (S&DA)

Bust of an unknown man
Hendrick de Keyser (Utrecht 1565–Amsterdam 1621), dated 1606
Polychrome terracotta; H. 72.5 cm, oak base H. 54 cm   (S&DA)

(top)
River landscape with wild boar hunt
Joos de Momper (Antwerp 1564–Antwerp 1635), *c* 1610
Panel; 121 × 196.5 cm   (PC)

Item from the wreck of 'De Witte Leeuw' (The White Lion)
The White Lion, an East Indiaman, went down in 1613 off St Helena with a cargo consisting mainly of pepper and porcelain.   (DH)

Still life with flowers
Jan Brueghel I (Brussels 1568–Antwerp 1625), *c* 1610
Copper; 24.5 × 19 cm   (PC)

(right)
Memorial Jug
Adam van Vianen (Utrecht 1569–Utrecht 1627), Utrecht, 1614
Gilded silver; H. 25.5 cm
Made for the Amsterdam Gold- and Silversmiths' Guild in memory of the silversmith Paulus van Vianen (*c*1570–Prague, 1613).   (S&DA)

70

Relief: Bacchus finding Ariadne on Naxos
Adriaen de Vries (The Hague 1546–Prague 1626), *c* 1610
Bronze; H. 52.5 cm, W. 42 cm   (S&DA)

Stand-up collar
Italy, 1st quarter 17th century
Reticella needlepoint on linen;
47 × 42 cm   (S&DA)

Dish with the story of Diana and Actaeon
Paulus van Vianen (Utrecht *c* 1570 –Prague 1613), 1613
Silver; 52 × 40.8 cm   (S&DA)

Fishing for souls'
Adriaen van de Venne (Delft 1589 – The
Hague 1662), 1614
Panel; 98 × 189 cm
An allegory of the jealousy between the
various religious denominations during the
Twelve Years Truce between the Dutch
Republic and Spain. (DH)

The fête champêtre
Esaias van de Velde (Amsterdam 1591–
The Hague 1630), 1615
Panel; 35 × 61 cm (PC)

Dignified couples courting
Willem Pietersz Buytewech (Rotterdam
1591/92–Rotterdam 1624), 1616/17
Canvas; 56 × 70 cm   (PC)

Winter landscape with ice skaters
Hendrick Avercamp (Amsterdam 1585–
Kampen 1634), 1618
Panel; 77.5 × 132 cm   (PC)

River valley
Hercules Seghers (Haarlem? 1589/90–in
or before 1638), 1615/20
Panel; 30 × 53.5 cm   (PC)

73

The adoration of the Magi
Hendrick ter Brugghen (Deventer 1588–Utrecht 1629), 1619
Canvas; 134 × 160 cm (PC)

The cattle ferry
Esaias van de Velde (Amsterdam 1591–The Hague 1630), 1622
Panel; 75.5 × 113 cm (PC)

Two salt cellars
Adam van Vianen (Utrecht 1569–Utrecht 1627), Utrecht, 1620 and 1621
Silver; H. 26 cm
One shows Cain and Abel, the other Abraham preparing to sacrifice his son. (S&DA)

(left)
Rummer with diamond engraving
Anna Roemers (Amsterdam 1583–Amsterdam 1651), dated 1621
Clear dark green glass; H. 13 cm, Diam. 6 cm
On the bowl a dragonfly, carnation, wild rose, marigold and shell and the inscription 'Bella Dori gentil, Noi Vaghi fron Da te prendiam gli honori'. Signed: Anna Roemers, Anno 1621. (S&DA)

Wedding portrait of Isaac Abrahamsz Massa and Beatrix van der Laen
Frans Hals (Antwerp 1581/85–Haarlem 1666), *c* 1622
Canvas; 140 × 166.5 cm (PC)

The merry fiddler
Gerard van Honthorst (Utrecht 1590–
Utrecht 1656), 1623
Canvas; 108 × 89 cm   (PC)

Kitchen scene
Alejandro de Loarte (active in Toledo
d. 1626), *c* 1625
Canvas; 100 × 122 cm   (PC)

An outdoor party
Dirck Hals (Haarlem 1591–Haarlem
1656), 1627
Panel; 78 × 137 cm   (PC)

**Tobias accusing Anna of stealing
the kid**
Rembrandt Harmensz van Rijn (Leiden
1606–Amsterdam 1669), 1626
Panel; 39.5 × 30 cm   (PC)

**Prometheus being chained by
Vulcan**
Dirck van Baburen (Utrecht 1590/95–
Utrecht 1624), 1623
Canvas; 202 × 184 cm   (PC)

The harbour of Middelburg
Adriaen van de Venne (Delft 1589–The
Hague 1662), 1625
Panel; 64 × 134 cm   (PC)

(left)
Democritus
Hendrick ter Brugghen (Deventer 1588–
Utrecht 1629), 1628
Canvas; 85.5 × 70 cm   (PC)

(right)
Heraclitus
Hendrick ter Brugghen (Deventer 1588–
Utrecht 1629), 1627
Canvas; 85.5 × 70 cm   (PC)

Self portrait
Rembrandt Harmensz van Rijn (Leiden
1606–Amsterdam 1669), 1628
Panel; 22.6 × 18.7 cm   (PC)

Dish with ship being attacked by a monster
Northern Netherlandish School, 1st half
17th century
Majolica; Diam. 33.8 cm (S&DA)

The merry drinker
Frans Hals (Antwerp 1581/85–Haarlem
1666), 1628/30
Canvas; 81 × 66.5 cm (PC)

Vanitas still life
School of Rembrandt, *c* 1630
Panel; 91 × 120 cm (PC)

Old woman reading a lectionary
Gerard Dou (Leiden 1613–Leiden 1675), *c* 1630
Panel; 71 × 55.5 cm (PC)

(top)
Jeremiah lamenting the destruction of Jerusalem
Rembrandt Harmensz van Rijn (Leiden 1606–Amsterdam 1669),
1630
Panel; 58 × 46 cm (PC)

(left)
The prophetess Anna
Rembrandt Harmensz van Rijn (Leiden 1606–Amsterdam 1669),
1631
Panel; 60 × 48 cm (PC)

The stone bridge
Rembrandt Harmensz van Rijn (Leiden 1606–Amsterdam 1669),
c 1638
Panel; 29.5 × 42.5 cm   (PC)

Portrait of a man
Frans Hals (Antwerp 1581/85–Haarlem 1666), *c* 1632
Canvas; 79.5 × 66.5 cm
Possibly a portrait of Nicolaes Hasselaer.   (PC)

Isaac blessing Jacob
Govert Flinck (Kleve 1615–Amsterdam
1660), 1638
Canvas; 117 × 141 cm   (PC)

Cabinet
Antwerp, 1st half of 17th century (stand 2nd half 17th century)
Various woods; H. 159 cm, W. 109 cm, D. 49.5 cm
The cabinet is of limewood, veneered with ebony and decorated with silver mounting. The stand is of oak veneered with ebonised walnut. The paintings show scenes from Genesis and are attributed to Frans Francken II (Antwerp 1581 – 1642).   (S&DA)

Still life with flowers
Hans Bollongier (Haarlem *c* 1600– Haarlem after 1645), 1639
Panel; 68 × 54.5 cm   (PC)

Pocket-watch
France, *c*1641
Enamelled gold case; Diam. 6.4 cm
The watch is decorated with allegories on the marriage of William II to Mary Stuart in 1641, painted by Henry Toutin of Blois. The mechanism is signed 'Antoine Masurier à Paris'.   (S&DA)

Scent bottle
Amsterdam or The Hague, *c* 1630
Enamelled gold with rubies; H. 5.1 cm
   (S&DA)

The whale-oil factory on Jan Mayen Island
Cornelis de Man (Delft 1621–Delft 1706), 1639
Canvas; 108 × 205 cm   (DH)

Two salt cellars
Johannes Lutma (Emden 1587–Amsterdam 1669), Amsterdam, 1639
Silver, partly gilded; H. 23.4 cm   (S&DA)

Maria Trip
Rembrandt Harmensz van Rijn (Leiden 1606–Amsterdam 1669), 1639
Panel; 107 × 82 cm   (PC)

The company of Captain Frans Banning Cocq and Lieutenant Willem van Ruytenburch: 'The Night Watch'
Rembrandt Harmensz van Rijn (Leiden 1606–Amsterdam 1669), 1642
Canvas; 363 × 437 cm (PC)

Oak cabinet
North Holland, 2nd quarter 17th century
Oak decorated with ebony; H. 212 cm, W. 160 cm, D. 78 cm
The figures represent Faith, Hope and Charity; the reliefs illustrate the story of Susanna. (S&DA)

Portrait of a girl in blue
Johannes Verspronck (Haarlem 1597–
Haarlem 1662), 1641
Canvas; 82 × 66.5 cm   (PC)

'The Night Watch' (detail)
Rembrandt Harmensz van Rijn (Leiden
1606–Amsterdam 1669), 1642

Landscape with two oaks
Jan van Goyen (Leiden 1596–The Hague
1656), 1641
Canvas; 88.5 × 110.5 cm   (PC)

Helena van der Schalcke (1646–1671)
Gerard ter Borch (Zwolle 1617–Deventer 1681), 1648
Panel; 34 × 28.5 cm   (PC)

Nassau armorial coat
Embroidered silk; c 1647
Worn at the funerals of Frederik Hendrik (1584–1647) and Prince
Willem IV (1711–1751).   (DH)

Jug and dish with maritime scenes
Johannes Lutma (Emden 1587–
Amsterdam 1669), Amsterdam, 1647
*Silver; H. 50.4 cm (jug), Diam. 70 cm
(dish)*
The arms of Cornelis Tromp were added
later (in or after 1676).   (S&DA)

(right)
**The celebration of the Peace of
Münster in the headquarters of the
St George's Guard, Amsterdam**
Bartholomeus van der Helst (Haarlem
1613–Amsterdam 1670), 1648
Canvas; 232 × 547 cm   (PC)

Still life with beer glass
Jan van de Velde (Haarlem 1619/20–
Enkhuizen 1662), 1647
Panel; 64 × 59 cm   (PC)

Interior of the St Odolphus church in Assendelft
Pieter Saenredam (Assendelft 1597–Haarlem 1665), *c* 1649
Panel; 50 × 76 cm   (PC)

Two horses in a meadow
Paulus Potter (Enkhuizen 1625–Amsterdam 1654), 1649
Panel; 23.5 × 30 cm   (PC)

Dish with landscape decoration
Delft, dated 1650
Earthenware; Diam. 37 cm   (S&DA)

(left)
River landscape with cattle ferry
Salomon van Ruysdael (Haarlem 1600/03–Haarlem 1670), 1649
Canvas; 99.5 × 133.5 cm   (PC)

River landscape in winter
Aert van der Neer (Amsterdam 1603/04–Amsterdam 1677),
c 1650
Canvas; 64 × 79 cm   (PC)

Peasants in an interior: 'The skaters'
Adriaen van Ostade (1610–1685), 1650
Panel; 44 × 35.5 cm   (PC)

The threatened swan
Jan Asselijn (Dieppe 1610–Amsterdam
1652), 1650
Canvas; 144 × 171 cm
Interpreted later as an allegory on Johan
de Witt. (PC)

**Reconstructed model of the East
Indiaman 'Prins Willem', fully
rigged**
Built by Herman Ketting, Rijksmuseum
restorer, 1979
Mainly wood; L. 130 cm
The taffrail (rail around the stern) is
decorated with the arms of the Chamber
of Middelburg, 1651. The Prins Willem
was probably the largest ship with taffrail
built in the 17th century for the Dutch
East Indies Company. During the first
Anglo-Dutch War it was converted to a
warship and served as Admiral Witte de
With's flag-ship. (DH)

**The home fleet saluting the state
barge**
Jan van de Cappelle (Amsterdam 1626–
Amsterdam 1679), 1650
Panel; 64 × 92.5 cm (PC)

The great hall of the Binnenhof, The Hague, during the great assembly of the States General in 1651
Dirck van Delen (Heusden 1605–
Arnemuiden 1671), 1651
Panel; 52 × 66 cm (DH)

Italian landscape with draftsman
Jan Both (Utrecht *c* 1615–Utrecht 1652),
c 1651
Canvas; 187 × 240 cm (PC)

Winter scene
Jan van de Cappelle (Amsterdam 1626–
Amsterdam 1679), 1652/53
Canvas; 51.5 × 67.4 cm (PC)

91

(right)
River landscape with riders
Aelbert Cuyp (Dordrecht 1620–
Dordrecht 1691), *c* 1655
Canvas; 128 × 227.5 cm   (PC)

**Interior of the Oude Kerk (Old
Church) in Delft**
Gerrit Houckgeest (The Hague *c* 1600–
Bergen op Zoom 1661), *c* 1654
Panel; 49 × 41 cm   (PC)

**Princess Henrietta Maria Stuart
(1631–1660)**
Bartholomeus van der Helst (Haarlem
1613–Amsterdam 1670), 1652
Canvas; 199.5 × 170 cm
Princess Henrietta Maria was the widow
of Willem II, Prince of Orange.   (PC)

**Gallant conversation: 'The paternal
admonition'**
Gerard ter Borch (Zwolle 1617–Deventer
1681), *c* 1654
Canvas; 71 × 73 cm   (PC)

Old woman in prayer: 'Prayer without end'
Nicolaes Maes (Dordrecht 1634–
Amsterdam 1693), c 1655
Canvas; 134 × 113 cm   (PC)

Girl at a window: 'The daydreamer'
Nicolaes Maes (Dordrecht 1634–
Amsterdam 1693), c 1655
Canvas; 123 × 96 cm   (PC)

Justitia
Artus Quellinus the Elder (Antwerp
1609–Antwerp 1668), *c*1650/57
Terracotta; H. 88 cm
Study for a larger-than-life-size bronze
statue for the façade of the former
Amsterdam Town Hall, now the Royal
Palace.   (S&DA)

**Distant view, with cottages lining a
road**
Philips Koninck (Amsterdam 1619–
Amsterdam 1688), *c*1655
Canvas; 133 × 167.5 cm   (PC)

**The anatomy lesson of Dr Joan
Deyman**
Rembrandt Harmensz van Rijn (Leiden
1606–Amsterdam 1669), 1656
Canvas; 100 × 134 cm   (PC)

94

The kitchen maid
Johannes Vermeer (Delft 1632–Delft
1675), *c* 1658
Canvas; 45.5 × 41 cm   (PC)

**View of houses in Delft: 'The little
street'**
Johannes Vermeer (Delft 1632–Delft
1675), *c* 1658
Canvas; 54.3 × 44 cm   (PC)

**The castle of Batavia, seen from Kali
Besar West**
Andries Beeckman (active in Deventer
between 1651–1657), 1656
Canvas; 108 × 151.5 cm   (DH)

Woman at her toilet
Jan Steen (Leiden 1626–Leiden 1679),
c 1660
Panel; 37 × 27.5 cm   (PC)

(top right)
Still life with silver jug
Willem Kalf (Amsterdam 1619–
Amsterdam 1693), *c* 1660
Canvas; 71.5 × 62 cm   (PC)

The feast of St Nicholas
Jan Steen (Leiden 1626–Leiden 1679),
c 1660
Canvas; 82 × 70.5 cm   (PC)

St Peter's denial
Rembrandt Harmensz van Rijn (Leiden
1606–Amsterdam 1669), 1660
Canvas; 154 × 169 cm   (PC)

**Titus van Rijn, Rembrandt's son, in
a monk's habit**
Rembrandt Harmensz van Rijn (Leiden
1606–Amsterdam 1669), 1660
Canvas; 79.5 × 67.7 cm   (PC)

Self portrait as the apostle Paul
Rembrandt Harmensz van Rijn (Leiden
1606–Amsterdam 1669), 1661
Canvas; 91 × 77 cm   (PC)

Woman reading a letter
Johannes Vermeer (Delft 1632–Delft
1675), 1662/63
Canvas; 46.5 × 39 cm   (PC)

**The wardens of the Amsterdam
drapers' guild**
Rembrandt Harmensz van Rijn (Leiden
1606–Amsterdam 1669), 1661
Canvas; 191.5 × 279 cm   (PC)

Interior with women beside a linen chest
Pieter de Hooch (Rotterdam 1629–
Amsterdam after 1683), 1663
Canvas; 72 × 77.5 cm (PC)

Still life
Abraham van Beyeren (The Hague 1620/
21–Overschie 1690), *c* 1665
Canvas; 126 × 106 cm (PC)

Cabinet
North Netherlandish School (?), 3rd
quarter 17th century
*Oak and ebony with intarsia and
marquetry of engraved mother-of-pearl; H.
222.5 cm, W. 206 cm, D. 84 cm* (S&DA)

The watermill
Meindert Hobbema (Amsterdam 1638–
Amsterdam 1709), *c* 1665
Panel; 62 × 85.5 cm   (PC)

The sick child
Gabriël Metsu (Leiden 1629–Amsterdam
1667), *c* 1665
Canvas; 32.2 × 27.2 cm   (PC)

The sick woman
Jan Steen (Leiden 1626–Leiden 1679),
c 1665
Canvas; 76 × 63.5 cm   (PC)

(right)
**The factory of the Dutch East India
Company in Houghly, Bengal**
Hendrik van Schuylenburgh (? *c* 1620–
Middelburg 1689), 1665
Canvas; 203 × 316 cm   (DH)

The love letter
Johannes Vermeer (Delft 1632–Delft
1675), *c* 1666
Canvas; 44 × 38.5 cm   (PC)

Boatmen moored on the shore of an Italian lake
Adam Pijnacker (Pijnacker *c* 1622 – Delft
1673), 1668
Canvas on panel; 97.5 × 85.5 cm   (PC)

The council of war on board 'De Zeven Provinciën', the flagship of Michiel Adriaensz de Ruyter, 10 June 1666 (detail)
Willem van de Velde I (Leiden *c* 1611–
London 1693), 1666
Canvas; 117 × 175 cm   (DH)

The arms of Great Britain
England, mid-17th century
Wood, polychrome
Part of the taffrail of the 'Royal Charles',
an English ship of the line captured by De
Ruyter and De Wit en route to Chatham.

(DH)

(right)
Rapier and sheath
Neapolitan, *c*1676
*Iron, red coral, copper, leather;
L. 104.8 cm*
Presented to Michiel Adriaenszoon de
Ruyter (1607–1676) in 1676 by the
Spanish Marquis de los Veles, Viceroy of
Naples, after De Ruyter had removed
the threat to Naples posed by the
French fleet.   (DH)

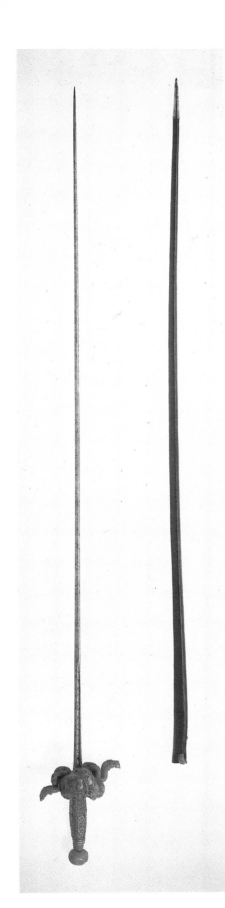

(top)
Portrait of a couple: 'The Jewish bride'
Rembrandt Harmensz van Rijn (Leiden 1606–Amsterdam 1669),
c 1667
Canvas; 121.5 × 166.5   (PC)

The merry family
Jan Steen (Leiden 1626–Leiden 1679), *c* 1670
Canvas; 110.5 × 141 cm   (PC)

104

In the last quarter of the seventeenth century, French taste gradually began to dominate in the Netherlands. In painting, the chiaroscuro effects of Rembrandt and his followers gave way to clear colours; simple clothing became more elaborate, often with the powdered wig that both monarch and merchant found in keeping with his status when his portrait was being painted. No mysterious shadows, but full light for personages who perhaps had more to hide than many of those half hidden in the darkness of Rembrandt's portraits. Ladies of high rank, both young and not so young, had themselves painted as shepherdesses or nymphs in mildly erotic conversation with young, robust shepherds, or chased by grinning satyrs. The houses of the patriciate were decorated with paintings in pastel tints portraying gods and goddesses on their divine thrones on Olympus or classical heroes in their palaces. In the stately Muses and their leader Apollo one can sometimes recognise the merchant with his wife and daughters. The paintings were done on the ceiling or set in the walls above the wainscotting as beautifully framed wall panels. Sometimes they depict park-like landscapes, the view of Arcadia which they preferred to that of the houses opposite.

Gerard Lairesse of Liège settled first in 's-Hertogenbosch, then in Utrecht and finally came to Amsterdam where he died in 1711, having been blind for the last twenty years of his life. He was an academic, a theoretician and the author of 'Het Groot Schilderboek' (Book of Great Painters), which explains the classical rules of painting and condemns the style of Rembrandt and his followers. De Lairesse was a creditable painter but opinion of him has certainly been unfavourably influenced by his criticism of Rembrandt. A good example of his talent is *Cleopatra's banquet* (p. 115) which demonstrates that he excels at everything of which an academic painter should be the master – anatomy, composition, opulence, expression, light, the correct costume (according to the ideas of the times) and architecture. The painting depicts the moment when Cleopatra dissolves a pearl in her wine in order to win the wager that she could provide the most expensive meal.

The old times, however, were not yet dead. Around 1680, Melchior d'Hondecoeter painted *The floating feather*: ducks, a pelican, a cassowary, a crane and other birds near a pool in a park (p. 115). Although this picture breathes the opulence of the wealthy

Part of a twelve-leaved Coromandel lacquer screen
China, 2nd half 17th century
Coromandel lacquer; H. 320 cm, W. 640 cm
One side shows Europeans, possibly Dutchmen, hunting in a Chinese landscape, the other side shows a pair of phoenix surrounded by trees, flowers and rocks on a gold background. (S&DA)

landowner, its artistic qualities – the fine reproduction of texture, the chiaroscuro effects and the subtle colouring – are part of the tradition established in the best years of the Golden Age. The same is true of the *Interior of the Portuguese synagogue in Amsterdam* by Emanuel de Witte (p.114). De Witte lived in various towns before settling in Amsterdam where he lived from 1652 until his death in 1692. He earned his fame as an architectural painter, but also painted markets and other similar scenes. His interiors of houses and churches are distinguished by their powerful chiaroscuro effects, geometric constructions which heighten perspective and the sober use of colour with occasional bright touches such as, in this painting, the blue of the man's coat to the left of centre.

The Dutch tradition of the observation of nature continued as late as 1690. Willem van de Velde the Younger painted *The gust of wind* in such a lifelike way that one can almost hear the wind whistling through the rigging, and the foam on the wave tops almost flies in the face of the spectator (p.118). The picture was to appeal strongly to nineteenth-century Romantic painters.

However, European politics and culture found no echo in the paintings of van de Velde, nor those of d'Hondecoeter, or even of Gerard Lairesse, who nevertheless was an adherent of the latest ideas. France dominated political and cultural life. Louis XIV, the Sun King, was on the throne, a despotic ruler who cherished ambitious plans for France in Europe. He gave his power outward expression by appointing many talented painters to his court and offering them important commissions. Visitors to Versailles can observe the results of Louis' plans for the expansion and furnishing of his palace there and the creation of spacious gardens with hundreds of statues and wonderful fountains. Louis XIV did even more, however. In 1662 he ordered the merger and expansion of the tapestry weavers to create the Gobelin factory, headed by the painter Charles Le Brun, who also managed and coordinated the decoration of the palace of Versailles. The King and his family, the court dignitaries, the nobles and high officials frequently had their portraits painted and they all commissioned paintings and tapestries showing historical, mythological or allegorical scenes. Everything was large and dazzling – in short on a royal scale.

In 1672 the Republic found itself engaged in mortal combat with the France it had so admired for its culture. In that year France, allied with England and two German states, invaded the Netherlands and her troops marched deep into the country, to Utrecht and beyond. Prince William III was proclaimed stadholder, and eventually his dynastic connections placed William on the English throne, after he had managed to oust James II in 1689. From that moment on he was both king and stadholder. The events of 1672 had far-reaching effects on the lives of Dutch citizens. The famous portrait painter Bartholomeus van der Helst went bankrupt and along with him many others. Since the French invasion Johannes Vermeer had been afflicted by serious financial problems, which probably hastened his death on 15 December 1675. Documents survive which tell the sorry story of his anxiety-ridden last years, full of debts, sales of property and the pawning of his possessions.

The style of the French, however, or rather of Louis XIV, continued to permeate many European countries, including the Netherlands, and acquired innumerable imitators. Only a small number of painters were still concerned with simple, common subjects, such as the interior of a farmhouse, a Dutch landscape with local peasantry or a still life with some rough pottery, flowers, a glass of wine, a basket of fruit and other everyday objects. Once again we are confronted with the fact that art has no difficulty in crossing borders disputed by hostile armies. Even William III, King and Stadholder and no friend of France, succumbed to the overwhelming splendour of French architecture and gardens when he had a splendid country house built near Apeldoorn at the end of the seventeenth century. It was built under the direction of the architect Jacob Roman and probably according to plans drawn up by the Académie d'Architecture in Paris, with interior decoration and a park designed by Daniel Marot, a Huguenot who had fled to the Netherlands. This palace, known as Het Loo, and its park were recently restored and reconstructed at enormous cost. Het Loo constitutes a lovely reflection of the grandeur of the court of Louis XIV, but nothing of the essence of the Dutch Republic.

King William was not the only one to come under the influence of the Louis XIV style: both the regents and the wealthy merchants wished to surround themselves with the modern art of the day. Even Nicolaes Maes, a pupil of Rembrandt's who was earlier described as an introspective painter, reversed direction entirely to follow the fashion and paint lighthearted portraits in the new style. He produced attractive works, but they lacked the authenticity and native character of seventeenth-century Dutch painting.

Around 1700 a remarkable piece of furniture was constructed (p.116). It is a dolls' house, made from a large cabinet, which was furnished as a house with several floors but no façade, so that the interior is visible. Dolls' houses were usually made by amateurs and few are of so high a standard as this one, which was the joint effort of several notable artists. It is an authentic historical document which records in detail the interior of a patrician home on the threshold of the eighteenth century.

The sober interiors of middle-class houses, simple and full of light as portrayed by Vermeer, de Hooch and others, were slowly becoming more luxurious. They held a greater number of objects which themselves were more decorative: silver jugs and dishes, foreign porcelain and table services as well as the most beautiful specimens of Delftware and groups of figures in porcelain, the speciality of the factories in Meissen and Sèvres. Walls, as remarked upon earlier, were covered with paintings in beautifully moulded frames and the furniture had the same elegant lines as the clothes made of costly materials which were worn by the ladies and gentlemen who lived in these houses. A very attractive form of ornamentation was marquetry, an inlaid veneer consisting usually of thin pieces of different types of wood, but often also of copper, tin, tortoiseshell and other materials, set in various patterns (p.113).

At the beginning of the eighteenth century interest in exotic objects reached a height, particularly in 'chinoiserie' (borrowings from Chinese art), although art from other faraway places had its devotees too. Chinese art became known in Europe mainly through the paintings on Chinese porcelain, a very expensive item which had been imported since the seventeenth century, since at that time porcelain was not made in Europe. Feverish attempts were made to learn the secret of its manufacture, and this was finally discovered by the chemist and alchemist Johan Friedrich Böttger, who had been provided with facilities at the castle of Augustus the Strong, Elector of Saxony, to make gold. Instead, he produced porcelain, having discovered the vital element – kaolin or China clay, which Saxony had in abundance.

In 1710 the Albrechtsburch in Meissen, Saxony, was converted into a porcelain factory. Within a very short time it became evident that porcelain was indeed 'gold', an extremely profitable commodity. Certainly the Elector and his advisers exhibited great perspicacity when they appointed the best designers, modellers and technicians to work on the production of porcelain. The reputation of Meissen porcelain rests not only on the very fine materials of which it is made, but also on the artistic qualities of its moulding and decoration, which are of the highest standard (p.113, p.115). Porcelain factories were later set up elsewhere, the most famous being at Höchst and Sèvres. They were not established in the Netherlands until the late eighteenth century, when high quality porcelain was made at Weesp and Loosdrecht (p.122), often modelled on Chinese porcelain both in form and decoration.

The Louis XIV style was followed first by the Regency style and then by Rococo, or Louis XV style. Rococo was more elegant and less massive than the two preceding styles. Its most well-known characteristic is asymmetry, but curiously enough, this was less a feature in France than elsewhere. Rococo tended towards the lighthearted, the charming, even the sugary. Bastardised Rococo can still be found in confectionery, at fairgrounds and in fancy goods shops: an interesting phenomenon which should not, however, colour our view of the original. At its best, Rococo is a pleasure to behold, playful and inventive. A white marble Cupid, his finger to his lips, sums up everything that Rococo meant: sweetness, grace, absolute mastery of form in movement, taste and the allusion to love (p.120). The statue, which originally belonged to Mme de Pompadour, was by the sculptor Etienne-Marie Falconet, who also carved a mounted statue of Czar Peter the Great which stood in Leningrad. He was appointed by Louis XV to supervise the quality of Sèvres porcelain and its decoration.

The Netherlands boasted no internationally known artists in the eighteenth century. Nevertheless, Cornelis Troost was a first-rate, versatile painter who was a master of both pastels and oils. His subjects, and his models, came from high society and the theatre, the subjects usually eighteenth-century farces by authors such as Thomas Asselijn, one of the most successful writers of comedy of the period (p.121). An exception to his usually satirical work, however, is the glimpse of the sunny garden behind a gentleman's house (p.116) and Troost also painted serious portraits, both of individuals and groups.

German art was of much higher quality in this period. Numerous substantial buildings were being constructed there: churches, royal residences and abbeys, the latter mainly in the Roman Catholic states, such as Franconia, whose capital was Würzburg. Baroque came to Germany from Italy, and Italian, German and Austrian artists painted huge, decorative frescos on walls and ceilings and in the interior of cupolas, creating the impression that one was looking directly into the heavens, where the gods sat at table. The great composer and organist Johann Sebastian Bach was a contemporary of the Baroque painters and architects, and they created the background against which his works were played.

The requirements of the nobility with regard to furnishing and decorating their houses gave rise to a flourishing industry. The elegance, lustre, colour and function of their furnishings would suggest that it was a peaceful society, but the four elegant legs of the writing table belonging to the Elector of Trier – to give just one example (p. 119) – are firmly planted, as it were, in the bustle of the times. The second half of the eighteenth century witnessed the decline of Hapsburg power under Empress Maria Theresa, the rise of the Kingdom of Prussia and constant changes in the alliances between the small states which made up the German Empire.

An unusual collection from a wealthy burgher's house in Haarlem dating from around 1790 illustrates the appearance of the interior of a rich man's house around the end of the century. The sober, taut lines, subtle shading in light green, white and blue-grey, and the return of classical motifs such as acanthus tendrils and ornamental patterns of winding lines (p. 125) are typical of the period when the Louis XVI style was dominant. The furniture was probably designed by the architect Abraham van der Hart, who also designed the Maagdenhuis on the Spui, Amsterdam, which now houses part of the University of Amsterdam.

The eighteenth century is in no way the characterless, complacent period it was for long thought to have been in the Netherlands. New ideas flourished in the fields of philosophy, politics and science; the Industrial Revolution got under way, the American colonies declared their independence and the Frenc' monarchy succumbed to the Revolution. The new ideals o freedom and quality were soon engulfed in blood and violence, but they survived to resurface time and again in the nineteenth century.

View of Haarlem
Jacob van Ruisdael (Haarlem 1628/29–
Amsterdam 1682), *c* 1670
Canvas; 43 × 38 cm   (PC)

The windmill at Wijk bij Duurstede
Jacob van Ruisdael (Haarlem 1628/29–
Amsterdam 1682), *c* 1670
Canvas; 83 × 101 cm   (PC)

(top)
Jug with Chinoiserie
'Het Moriaenshooft' pottery, from the
factory owned by Rochus Jacobsz
Hoppesteyn, Delft, *c* 1685
Earthenware; H. 25 cm   (S&DA)

Dish with Chinoiserie
Attributed to the pottery 'De Metalen
Pot', owned by Lambertus Cleffius, Delft,
c 1680
Earthenware; Diam. 40 cm   (S&DA)

(left)
**Dressing gown belonging to King
Willem III (1650–1702)**
2nd half 17th century
Silk; L. 154 cm   (DH)

(above)
Oak table leaf
Antwerp, 1689, signed and dated 'Peeter De Loose Sculsit 1689
Antverpiae' and 'Michiel Verbiest Fesit 1689'
Oak, veneered with tortoise-shell, copper, brass and mother-of-pearl;
88 × 148 cm
Inlaid with the arms of Simon de Neuf (1647–1714) and Jacoba
Martina van Eversdijck (d. 1711), who married in 1686.   (S&DA)

(top left)
Temple of Venus
Model by J.G. Kirchner (1706–after 1737), Meissen, 1727
Porcelain; H. 28.2 cm, W. 21.2 cm
In the centre Venus with Cupid, (*left*) Jupiter (*right*)
Juno.   (S&DA)

Oak cabinet
Attributed to Jan van Mekeren, Amsterdam, *c* 1700
Oak veneered with palisander, maple, palm, mahogany, walnut and
cherry; H. 205 cm, W. 173 cm, D. 61 cm   (S&DA)

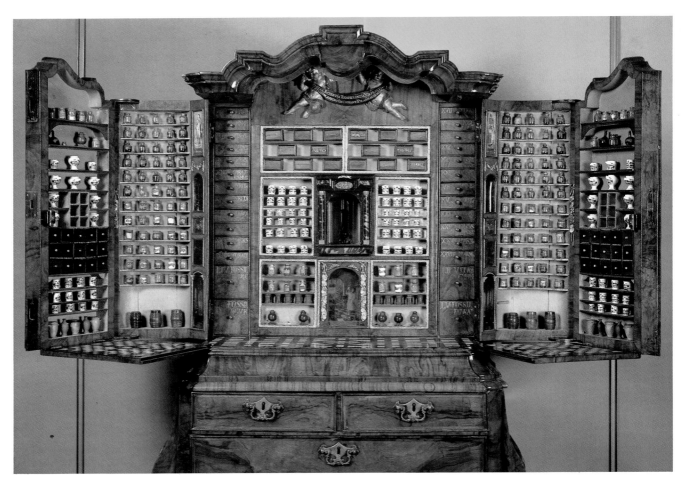

Simplicia cabinet (detail)
Northern Netherlandish School, dated
1730. The central niche originally
belonged to another piece of furniture
(2nd half 17th century).
*Oak, inlaid with burr walnut; H.
207.5 cm, W. 93 cm, D. 71.5 cm*
From the Collegium Medico-
Pharmaceuticum Delfensis (the Delft
Guild of Apothecaries) and used during
examinations. The original contents,
consisting of simple medicines (*simplicia*),
are still largely preserved in miniature
apothecaries' jars made of Delftware.

(S&DA)

**Interior of the Portuguese
synagogue in Amsterdam**
Emanuel de Witte (Alkmaar 1616/18–
Amsterdam 1692), 1680
Canvas; 110 × 99 cm   (PC)

Cleopatra's banquet
Gerard Lairesse (Lüttich 1641–
Amsterdam 1711), *c* 1680
Canvas; 74 × 95.5 cm   (PC)

Pelican and other birds near a pool:
'The floating feather'
Melchior d'Hondecoeter (Utrecht 1636–
Amsterdam 1695), *c* 1680
Canvas; 159 × 144 cm   (PC)

Madonna and child on crescent moon
Matthieu van Beveren (Antwerp 1630–
Brussels 1690), 1680/90
Ivory; H. 58 cm   (S&DA)

Vase with Höroldt chinoiserie on
purple background
Painted by J.G. Höroldt (1696–1775),
Meissen, *c* 1727
Porcelain; H. 39.8 cm   (S&DA)

115

An Amsterdam town garden
Cornelis Troost (Amsterdam 1696–
Amsterdam 1750), *c* 1745
Canvas; 66 × 56 cm   (PC)

Corner mantelpiece
Northern Netherlandish School, 1st quarter 18th century, in the
style of Daniel Marot (c 1661–1752)
*Red marbled mantel and green painted breast, decorated with gilded
carving, and with consoles for displaying porcelain; H. 300 cm, W.
158 cm, D. 86 cm*   (S&DA)

(left, above)
Child's costume
Mid 18th century
According to tradition this was worn by Willem V (1748–1806),
Prince of Orange-Nassau.   (DH)

(left)
Dolls' house (detail)
Amsterdam, *c* 1690
*Oak cabinet, veneered with tortoise-shell and tin; H. 255 cm,
W. 189.5 cm, D. 78 cm*
Made for Petronella Oortman, wife of Jan Brandt. The furnishings
are on the same scale and made with the same materials as they
would have been in a real house of the period.
Ground floor: show kitchen, working kitchen with toilet and cellar,
room with tapestries and library at rear. First floor: drawing room,
entrance hall with office above, lying-in room. Attic: attic and
servants' rooms, peat loft, nursery.   (S&DA)

Tile tableau, with Chinoiserie and Negroes
Delft, 1st quarter 18th century
Earthenware; 170 × 79 cm   (S&DA)

117

Antoinette Metayer (1732–1788)
George van der Mijn (London 1726/27–
Amsterdam 1763), 1759
Canvas; 63.5 × 49 cm   (PC)

**A ship on the high seas caught by a
squall: 'The gust of wind'**
Willem van de Velde II (Leiden *c* 1633–
London 1707), *c* 1690
Canvas; 77 × 63.5 cm   (PC)

**The uncompleted tower of the
Nieuwe Kerk and the rear façade of
the town hall, Amsterdam**
Isaak Ouwater (Amsterdam 1750–
Amsterdam 1793), 1780
Canvas; 59 × 73 cm   (PC)

(right)
Oak cabinet
Amsterdam, *c* 1780
Oak, veneered with mahogany; H. 300 cm, W. 282 cm, D. 80.5 cm
Includes numerous drawers intended for storing natural objects.
From the 'Natura Artis Magistra' Society in Amsterdam.   (S&DA)

Writing table
Abraham Roentgen (1711–1795) and David Roentgen (1743–1807), Neuwied, *c* 1765
Oak, maple and walnut, veneered with rosewood, ebony, palisander, satinwood and various other types of wood, tortoiseshell, silver, mother-of-pearl, copper and bone, with a mounting of fire-gilded bronze; H. 148.5 cm, W. 113 cm, D. 62 cm
According to the initials, arms and portrait medallion, made for Johann Philipp von Walderdorff, Elector and Archbishop of Trier.
(S&DA)

(top left)
Wall table
Designed by Giovanni Battista Piranesi (1720–1778), 1765
Carved and gilded limewood, with a top of green combed marble; H. 92 cm, W. 147 cm, D. 72 cm
Made for Cardinal Giovanni Battista Rezzonico, nephew of Pope Clement XIII.

Mirror
England, *c* 1760
Carved and gilded wood in Chippendale style; H. 240 cm, W. 105 cm

Panels
The Netherlands, 3rd quarter 18th century
Gilded leather with polychrome painting on gilded, embossed background, H. 263 cm
From Mon Plaisir House, Schuddebeurs near Zierikzee, Zeeland.
(S&DA)

119

Dish with Chinoiserie
Delft, 2nd quarter 18th century
Earthenware; Diam. 35 cm
(S&DA)

Wedding dress
France (?), mid 18th century
Light blue rep silk, embroidered in multi-coloured silk and consisting of a bodice with an attached train, skirt and separate train; H. 140.5 cm; W. 230 cm, waist 58 cm (skirt), L. 216.5 cm, W. 153.5 cm (loose train)
'Grand parure' (ie. a gala dress), since the skirt was worn over an extra wide crinoline (panier à coudes). Round lead weights are sewn into the sleeves. Worn in The Hague in 1759 by Helena Slicher (1737–1776) at her wedding to Aelbrecht Baron van Slingelandt (1731–1801). (S&DA)

Seated Cupid: 'Love threatens'
Etienne-Maurice Falconet (Paris 1716–Paris 1791), dated 1757
Marble; H. 87 cm, including base 185 cm
From the property of Mme de Pompadour. (S&DA)

120

Still life with flowers
Jan van Huysum (Amsterdam 1682–
Amsterdam 1740), *c* 1730
Canvas; 80.5 × 62 cm

Wine fountain and cooler
Alger Mensma (1682–after 1752),
Amsterdam. Reliefs attributed to Jan
Lanckhorst (1668–1744), 1731 and 1732
Silver; H. 50.8 cm (fountain), H. 23 cm,
W. 44.8 cm (cooler)
Commissioned as gifts from the Admiralty
of Amsterdam and the Dutch East Indies
Company to Captain Cornelis Schrijver.

(S&DA)

The spendthrift
Cornelis Troost (Amsterdam 1696–
Amsterdam 1750), 1741
Panel; 68.5 × 86 cm
A scene from Thomas Asselijn's play of
the same name. (PC)

Coffee jug, painted with flowers
Loosdrecht, *c* 1775/80
Porcelain; H. 23.1 cm   (S&DA)

Box with hunting scenes
Paris, *c* 1750
*Gold with translucent enamel; H. 4.6 cm,
D. 9.9 cm*   (S&DA)

Goblet with lid
Engraving by Jacob Sang,
Amsterdam, 1768
*Clear colourless glass; H. 28.9 cm, Diam.
10.3 cm*
The goblet is decorated with a view of a
lake and driveway and inscribed 'Ex undis'
and 'Renata Floreat'. Signed: 'Jacob Sang,
fec. Amsterdam 1768.'   (S&DA)

**Goblet, with the arms of the States
General and the flag of the United
States of America**
Probably English with Dutch engraving,
1782
Glass; H. 18.5 cm
Probably commissioned to mark the
recognition of the United States by the
States General on 19 April 1782.   (DH)

Satire on the extremely high hairstyle for ladies
Model by Johan Peter Melchior (1747–1825), *c* 1775
Porcelain; H. 27 cm, W. 19 × 35.3 cm   (S&DA)

Ice-pail decorated with birds in a landscape
Amstel, *c*1790/1800
Porcelain; H. 43.5 cm   (S&DA)

Tureen on an under-dish
Engelbart Joosten (1717–1789), The Hague, 1772
Silver; H. 29.3 cm, W. 34.5 cm (tureen); B. 58.5 cm, D. 37.5 cm (dish)
Engraved with the alliance arms of Assueer Jan Baron Torck and Eusebia Jacoba de Rode van Heeckeren, who married in 1758.
                                    (S&DA)

Cooler with engraved arms
Gregorius van der Toorn (1715–1768), The Hague, 1768
Silver; H. 29.6 cm, W. 63 cm
Probably the arms of the Hillebrandes family.   (S&DA)

Goblet
Louis Metayer (?–1774) and Philippe
Metayer (1697–1763), Amsterdam, 1754.
Reliefs based on a design by L.F.
Dubourg (1693–1775), dating from 1753
Gold; H. 24.5 cm
Probably made to mark the marriage of
Johan van Borssele and Anna Coninck in
1750. (S&DA)

**Tapestry: Cupid with two torches in
a medallion**
Paris, Gobelin Royal under Jacques
Neilson (signed), from a design by
François Boucher, and Maurice Jacques
and Louis Tessier (frame), between 1776
and 1784.
Wool and silk; 370 × 235 cm (S&DA)

(right)
Wainscotting and furniture
Northern Netherlandish School, *c* 1790
(wainscotting); French School, *c* 1790
(furniture)
*Wainscotting: painted oak and
softwood, with silk spanning. Furniture:
painted beech wood covered with figured
silk. H. 425 cm, L. 970 cm, W. 500 cm*
Made for Willem Ph. Kops' house at
Nieuwe Gracht 74, Haarlem, and probably
designed by Abraham van der Hart (1747–
1820). The furniture, curtains,
chandelier, lustres and carpet were made
for this room. (S&DA)

Tortoise-shell box
Made by Jean Saint (1698–1774) after a design by François Thuret (1716–after 1755),
1749
Mounted with moulded and chased gold and a fragment of gold ore; 18 × 11.5 × 5 cm
In this box, the charter of the Dutch West Indies Company was presented to
Prince Willem IV in 1749. (DH)

1790 to the present day

Between the French Revolution and the fall of Napoleon, the Netherlands were under French rule, first as a vassal state (the Batavian Republic), then as the Kingdom of Holland under Louis Napoleon and it was finally incorporated into the French Empire from 1810 to 1813. Art continued to flourish in this period, as shown by a painting by Adriaan de Lelie depicting the interior of a house belonging to the Amsterdam art collector Gildemeester (p. 133). King Louis Napoleon promoted the arts by awarding grants to promising artists – known as 'kwekelingen' or 'pensionnaires' – to complete their studies abroad, usually in Paris or Rome. During this period landscape painters in particular distinguished themselves by extremely pure and tightly constructed scenes of great clarity, which nonetheless expressed a great love of nature.

This was the period of the Empire style – in a sense a continuation of the Louis XVI style, but with the addition of Egyptian and Greek elements and shorn of its luxury, which was replaced by a touch of Spartan sobriety more suitable to the military style of government adopted by Emperor Napoleon. The Empire style is clearly evident in the silver jug from a service made for Grand Duke Nicholas (p. 134). The style of dress of the period can be seen in a magnificent group portrait of Rutger Jan Schimmelpenninck, Legate of the Batavian Republic in Paris, and his family (p. 126). The portrait was painted in Paris by Pierre-Paul Prud'hon, an artist whose figures, mostly shrouded in a vague poeticism, were in marked contrast to the work of his French contemporaries, such as Louis David, who practised a cool classicism.

After the liberation from France, the times remained turbulent for the Netherlands. The family of the stadholder returned from exile in England in 1813 and William Frederick, the eldest son of the previous stadholder William V, accepted sovereignty under the name of King William I (1814 – 1840). He had been preceded by a triumvirate which had prepared his return. A painting by Jan Willem Pieneman (p. 136) shows them meeting in the house of van Hogendorp, one of the triumvirate, preparatory to the assumption of power in the name of the Prince of Orange.

As every schoolchild knows, Napoleon returned to Europe and was defeated for the last time by the Allies at the Battle of

Rutger Jan Schimmelpenninck, Legate of the Batavian Republic in Paris, with his wife Catharina Nahuys and children Catharina and Gerrit
Pierre Paul Prud'hon (Cluny 1758–Paris 1823), 1801/02
Canvas; 263.5 × 200 cm   (DH)

Waterloo, near Brussels, in 1815. The Rijksmuseum possesses a painting of this world-shaking event by Jan Willem Pieneman (p.136). It portrays the moment in which the wounded Prince of Orange (the future William II) was borne from the battlefield. According to the evidence of the English commander, the Duke of Wellington, the Prince fought heroically and was partly responsible for holding back the French troops under Marshal Ney until the Prussians arrived. Wellington is the central figure in the painting. Pieneman had spent some time in the Duke's house in London painting portraits of Wellington and his principal officers, which he then incorporated in his giant canvas. The portrait, painted on Pieneman's own initiative, was eventually purchased by King William I as a present for his son and still belongs to the Royal Family.

In 1815 the Congress of Vienna decided that the Netherlands and Belgium should form one kingdom under William I. In 1830 the Belgians rebelled and demanded independence. The revolution was successful and Leopold I of Saxe-Coburg became the first King of Belgium. A notable episode from the Belgian Revolution was the heroic death of the Dutch Lieutenant van Speyk, who preferred to blow up his gunboat in Antwerp harbour rather than surrender to the Belgians (p.136). Van Speyk received a hero's funeral in the Nieuwe Kerk in Amsterdam.

The nineteenth century was a period in which people in the Netherlands looked back with respect to the past, particularly to the Golden Age. Thus there are numerous paintings depicting moments in the lives of famous men of that era, such as Hugo Grotius, Michiel de Ruyter, Tromp, Johan de Witt, stadholder Frederick Henry and the poet Vondel. Such scenes would indeed have been fascinating had they been painted by contemporaries. How interesting to see, for example, the famous composer and organist Jan Pietersz Sweelinck playing the organ in the Oude Kerk in Amsterdam, while the public wandered in and out. However, none of his contemporaries caught the moment for posterity – they obviously found such scenes too banal. Art is, after all, primarily dependent on the choice of the artist. It is a mirror of the times only in that it reflects the spirit of the artist.

The congenial, meticulous landscapes of Barend Cornelis Koekkoek (p.137) create an easy-going atmosphere in which the observer can enjoy the beauty of the countryside without feeling threatened by the forces of nature. For a painter like Koekkoek, the seasons are no longer the eternal natural cycle, but simply changes in nature's clothing. Nevertheless, this does not detract from the picturesque beauty, portrayed through the sensitive use of lighting effects, of Koekkoek's paintings.

In the first half of the nineteenth century a new mode of thought and feeling spread over Europe – the Romantic movement. One of the few exponents of the new style in the Netherlands was the landscape painter Wijnand Nuyen (1813–1839), who died extremely young. His *River landscape with ruin* (p.137) is a genuinely

Romantic picture and not a sentimental surrogate. The similarity in composition to Ruisdael's *Mill at Wijk bij Duurstede* (p.111) is striking, but whereas order and monumentality determine Ruisdael's vision, the wild, cloudy sky, the desolate castle, the chaotic vegetation on the river bank and the dramatic lighting convey Nuyen's view of nature as an overwhelming power in comparison to which man is an insignificance. This is, of course, an entirely Romantic idea.

The panorama of art was not, however, entirely dominated by Romanticism, although what are known as the 'neo-' styles originate from it. The image of nineteenth-century art is largely determined by such styles which, as the term indicates, were new applications of old styles, whether Renaissance, Gothic, Rococo or Roman. The return to old styles grew from a renewed interest in the European past, an interest which is one of the features of Romanticism, so that to some degree the neo- styles can indeed be seen as part of the Romantic movement.

There is no single example of Dutch art which demonstrates that the first half of the nineteenth century represented a total change from the previous period. Fortunately, however, the Rijksmuseum does have a magnificent specimen of the work of Goya, the Spanish painter who is considered to be one of the forerunners of modern art. This portrait (p.135) expresses not only the new philosophy which inspired artists, but also their altered attitude towards society. There is no trace of the subordination of the craftsman to his illustrious subject, but a free, personal interpretation of the latter's nature and appearance. Moreover, Goya does not follow any stereotyped pattern or prescription in his painting, but creates sudden irruptions of colour and light. It is hard to believe that Goya was initially a pupil of the Italian Tiepolo who produced High Baroque ceiling paintings for various palaces belonging to eighteenth-century nobility and church dignitaries. Goya had in fact withdrawn from that world where art was a confirmation of the power of its patron in a harrowing series of etchings entitled *The disasters of war*. Anyone who wishes for proof of Goya's ability to convey personality has only to compare his work with Neuman's portrait of the liberal Dutch statesman Thorbecke (p.137). While Goya's portrait of Judge Don Ramón Satué is distinguished by its spiritual qualities, the portrait of Thorbecke is distinguished only by the medal which he wears so proudly on his chest.

In the second half of the nineteenth century there was a revival of seventeenth-century Dutch landscape painting, but this cannot strictly be termed a 'neo-' style, since this suggests a revival of a style which has disappeared for one reason or another. The tradition of seventeenth-century landscape painting, on the contrary, had persisted in another form and was never interrupted. The English had always had great admiration for Dutch landscape paintings and drawings and amassed large collections of them. When a new style of park design developed in the eighteenth century, the landscape architects took their inspiration from Dutch paintings.

At the end of the century the Norwich School came into being, a school of aquarellists who went outside to paint the countryside as a whole. Up to then it had been the custom for painters to sketch motifs out of doors which they then worked up into a painting in the studio. The activities of the Norwich School therefore represented a radical innovation. However, since the scenes which they painted had mostly been 'improved' by landscape architects after the painted syle of Ruisdael, Hobbema and others, the spirit of Dutch landscape painting survived. Painters in oils rapidly mastered the art of painting 'on the spot' – John Constable is one of the most famous – and admiration for their works spread to France, where the Barbizon School was set up in the forest of Fontainebleau. It was the painters of this school who, in their turn, inspired Dutch landscape painters in the second half of the nineteenth century, thus completing the circle.

Most Dutch landscape painters in the second half of the nineteenth century belonged to the Hague School, although there were those who worked in The Hague who did not belong to it and those who lived and worked outside the city who did. But since the leaders of the movement, such as Mauve and the brothers Maris, actually did work in The Hague, the name has survived. It was also known as the 'grey' school, since a number of them at least were fond of heavy, cloudy skies and of thick layers of paint. Gerard Bilders of Utrecht was considered to be a 'real' Hague School artist (p. 138). The pasture with grazing cattle seen in Bilders' work was a favourite motif with the Hague School generally. There was no distinct division into foreground, middle distance and perspective. They painted nature in one piece with light as the unifying factor, as it is in reality. Another favourite motif is a river or canal flowing through a meadow into the distance, as painted in the sunlit scene by Weissenbruch (p. 138). Neither Bilders nor Weissenbruch can really be considered to be of the 'grey' school, although the name itself came from Weissenbruch, who spoke of the 'coloured grey' that he saw. Perhaps Anton Mauve best lives up to the name, with his subtle, pearly colours which contain a hint of grey even when he portrays a sunlit beach with horse riders (p. 139). There is a magnificent gloss on the horses' hides and the three lines of shadow under their bodies suffice to make the glow of the sun reverberate throughout the painting and emphasise the powdery nature of the sand.

Willem Maris, one of three brothers, said he was a painter not of cattle but of light. Or, it seems, sometimes of ducks (p. 140). The motif which seems so self-evident to us was completely new in Maris' time and more or less his own. It was as if he wished to narrow his vision down, as can be seen if one compares his few ducks on a piece of grass with, say, the panoramic vista painted by the seventeenth-century artist Philips Koninck (p. 94).

In addition to the Hague School, there was also a group of Impressionists working in Amsterdam, the leading lights of which were George Breitner and Isaac Israëls. Breitner painted the city of Amsterdam, usually in melting snow or drizzling rain, whereas

Israëls' work is lighter in mood. Breitner's *Bridge over the Singel* (p. 141) is a good example of his rough, masculine art, while *Donkey riding on the beach* (p. 141) sums up that of Israëls, the most French of the Dutch Impressionists.

The Hague School and the Amsterdam Impressionists were contemporary with the Impressionists in France, where the movement began. French Impressionism consisted entirely of light and colour: there were no shadows. Its most famous exponents are Claude Monet, Sisley, Renoir, Lautrec, Degas and Pissarro. Pointillism, a technique elaborated from Impressionism, and Post-Impressionism mark the end of the nineteenth century.

There are, of course, painters who do not really fit into any particular movement: such 'outsiders' include Vincent van Gogh and Paul Gaugin, although one could call the former an early Expressionist and Gaugin a Symbolist. About the time that van Gogh died in 1890, a new style was evolving, principally in Belgium, called simply Art Nouveau, or new art. It was characterised by decorative plant motifs and the absence of straight lines: all is flowing form. The style was used in architecture, the visual arts and arts and crafts between 1890 and 1910. Art Nouveau, or *Jugendstil* as it is known in Germany, also became popular in the Netherlands and was applied to all aspects of art, including ceramics. For a period of about ten years the vases and other objects made of Rozenburg pottery and porcelain (p. 142) enjoyed considerable fame. The factory was situated in The Hague and was in operation from 1883 to 1916. It flourished for only ten years because Art Nouveau had by that time been consigned to oblivion as other ideas and forms, such as Expressionism, Functionalism and abstract art which were in direct conflict with the naturalist/decorative philosophy of Art Nouveau, became popular. It is not Art which is subject to the whims of fashion, but rather its audience.

The Raamportje, Amsterdam
Wouter Johannes van Troostwijk (Amsterdam 1782–Amsterdam 1810), 1809
Canvas; 57 × 48 cm   (PC)

132

The art gallery of Jan Gildemeester Jansz in his house on the Herengracht, Amsterdam
Adriaan de Lelie (Tilburg 1755–Amsterdam 1820), 1794/95
Panel; 63.7 × 85.7 cm (PC)

Visit of the woman cherry pedlar
Abraham van Strij (Dordrecht 1753–Dordrecht 1826), 1816
Panel; 72.7 × 59 cm (PC)

Diorama: view of the square in Paramaribo and the governor's palace seen from the southwest during the British rule
G. Schouten (Amsterdam 1815–Amsterdam 1878), 1813
Paper; 68.5 × 99 ×32 cm (DH)

Goblet with stipple engraving
David Wolff (1732–1798), The Hague,
signed: D. Wolff, 1794
Clear colourless English glass;
H. 15.2 cm, Diam. 6.5 cm
The bowl is decorated with an allegory on
the visual arts (drawing and sculpture).

(S&DA)

A watercourse near 's-Graveland
Pieter Gerardus van Os (The Hague
1776–The Hague 1839), 1817
Panel; 111.5 × 89.5 cm   (PC)

**Part of a service made for Grand
Duke Nicholas, son of Paul I of
Russia**
Martin-Guillaume Biennais (1764–1843),
Paris, *c* 1809–19
Gilded silver; H. 33 cm (largest piece)

(S&DA)

(top right)
**The Gulf of Naples, with the island of Ischia in the
background**
Josephus Augustus Knip (Tilburg 1777–Berlicum 1847), 1818
Canvas; 90 × 109 cm   (PC)

**Maquette of the island of Deshima, the Dutch trading
settlement at Nagasaki, Japan**
Japan, before 1820
198 × 80 × 35.5 cm   (DH)

Don Ramon Satué (1765–1824)
Francisco de Goya y Lucientes (Fuendetodos 1746–Bordeaux
1828), 1823
Canvas; 107 × 83.5 cm   (PC)

**The Triumvirate assuming power in the name of the
Prince of Orange, 21 November 1813**
Jan Pieneman (Abcoude 1779–Amsterdam 1853), *c* 1828
Canvas; 70 × 86.5 cm   (DH)
(top)
The Battle of Waterloo
Jan Pieneman (Abcoude 1779–Amsterdam 1853), 1824
Canvas; 576 × 836 cm   (DH)

Winter landscape
Barend Koekkoek (Middelburg 1803–
Kleve 1862), *c* 1835
Canvas; 62 × 75 cm   (PC)

Johan Rudolf Thorbecke
Jan Hendrik Neuman (Cologne 1819–The
Hague 1898), 1852
Canvas; 100 × 84 cm
Thorbecke (1796–1872) was Minister of
State and Minister of the Interior.   (DH)

River landscape with ruins
Wijnand Nuyen (The Hague 1813–The
Hague 1839), 1836
Canvas; 99 × 141.5 cm   (PC)

(left)
**Jan van Speijk decides whether or
not to put the spark to the tinder,
5 February 1831**
Jacobus Schoemaker Doyer (Krefeld
1792–Zutphen 1867), *c* 1835
Canvas; 89 × 75 cm   (DH)

Cows in the meadow
Albert Bilders (Utrecht 1838–Amsterdam
1865), *c* 1861
Canvas; 47 × 70 cm   (PC)

The Zuiderhavendijk in Enkhuizen
Cornelis Springer (Amsterdam 1817–
Hilversum 1891), 1868
Panel; 50 × 65 cm   (PC)

View near the Geestbrug
Hendrik Weissenbruch (The Hague 1824–
The Hague 1903), 1868
Panel; 31 × 50 cm   (PC)

Morning ride on the beach
Anton Mauve (Zaandam 1838–Arnhem 1888), c 1876
Canvas; 45 × 70 cm   (PC)

Chinese vase
China, 1883
Silver; H. 86 cm
Presented to J.T. Cremer in 1883 by the planters of Deli-Langkat and Serdang. Jacob Theodor Cremer (1847–1923) was manager of the Deli Company from 1870 to 1883 and made a considerable contribution to the success of tobacco growing in East Sumatra.   (S&DA)

Horse artillery
George Hendrik Breitner (Rotterdam 1857–Amsterdam 1923), 1884/85
Canvas; 115 × 77.5 cm   (PC)

139

Ducks
Willem Maris (The Hague 1844–The
Hague 1910), 1885/90
Canvas; 93 × 113 cm   (PC)

**A windmill on a polder waterway: 'In
the month of July'**
Paul Gabriël (Amsterdam 1828–
Scheveningen 1903), 1888
Canvas; 102 × 66 cm   (PC)

The bridge over the Singel at Paleisstraat, Amsterdam
George Hendrik Breitner (Rotterdam 1857–Amsterdam 1923), 1890
Canvas; 100 × 152 cm   (PC)

Donkey riding on the beach
Isaac Israels (Amsterdam 1865–The Hague 1934), 1900/01
Canvas; 51 × 70 cm   (PC)

'Wystaria' pendant
Georges Fouquet (1862–1957), Paris, *c* 1900/10
Gold, enamel and baroque pearls; H. 10.8 cm, W. 6 cm
(S&DA)

Vase with lid, decorated with lilies
Décor by Samuel Schellink (1876–1958), The Hague, Rozenburg,
dated 1900
Porcelain; H. 59 cm (S&DA)

142

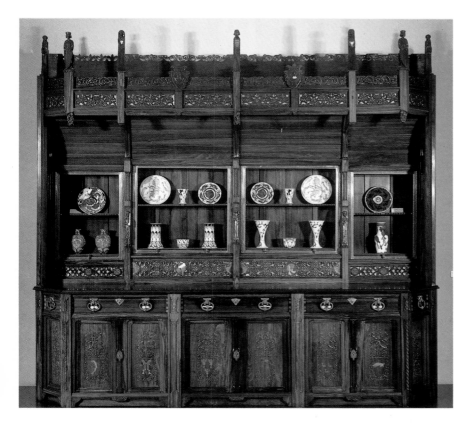

Sideboard
Made in the workshop of E.J. van Wisselingh & Co. from a design
by C.A. Lion Cachet (1864–1955), *c*1910
Coromandel, inlaid with palmwood, copper and ivory; H. 285 cm,
W. 306 cm, D. 79 cm
The three small sculptures on the uprights of the centre piece are
probably by J. Mendes da Costa (1863–1939). (S&DA)

Portrait of Dr W. Drees
W.M. Voois (Ter-Heyde aan de Zee), 1960
Shells; 26 × 29.5 cm
Willem Drees, a socialist born in Amsterdam on 3 July 1886, was
one of the most important statesmen of the post-war period in the
Netherlands. In 1957, while Minister for Social Affairs, he
introduced general old age pensions, which were to provide a basic
income for every Dutch citizen over sixty-five. The expression 'to
draw your Drees', meaning your pension, still survives today. The
shell portrait was made as a gift in 1960 by a sixty-five-year-old
admirer of Drees, W.M. Voois. Drees later presented it to the
Rijksmuseum. (DH)

Henricus Le viij. de ce nom/par la grace de Dieu Roy Dangleterre/z Dirlende/Prince de Wales/nasquist a Grienewicke trois lieues engloises de Londres/en lan de nostre Seigneur. M. CCCC. z. xc. en la sixiesme annee de henry le vij. Et commenceoit son Raigne le. xxij. iour Da= puril/en lan. M. CCCC. z. ix. z fut couronne a Westmunster sur la feste de la natiuite de. S. Iehan baptiste lan. M. D. z. xvij. il espousoit ma dame Ianne Seymer/de laquelle en lan. M. D. z. xxxvij. il gaigne Prince Edward/qui fut naiz a hamton court/sur la reille de S Edwarde. Auquel nostre Seigneur Dieu tout puissant vueille octroier victoire/puis/z honneur. Amen.

DIEV EST MON DROIT

HONY · SOYT · QVI · MAL · Y · PENSE ·

Imprime en Anuers sur la rue de Lombaers au lieurier blansch/par moy Iehan Liefrinck Tailleur de Figures.

144

The Print Room

The Print Room is a rather unusual section of the Rijksmuseum in that the prints, drawings, watercolours and other works on paper which are kept here are too fragile to be permanently exposed to the light and are therefore stored in portfolios and boxes. Visitors who have some special interest in them may ask to see them in the study room, but exhibitions of items drawn from the vast collection (about a million works) take place throughout the year in rooms 128–133, immediately next to the right-hand main entrance.

The Print Room houses the Netherlands' national print collection and the emphasis is therefore on Dutch artists, examples of whose work have been collected from all periods up to 1940. Rembrandt's etchings are almost all here: together with the innumerable states (proofs) and variants of each subject they amount to 1200 items. Other treasures include the extremely rare prints of Hercules Seghers (p.149) – with 75 items the Print Room has the largest collection of his work. There are also roughly the same number of prints by an unnamed late medieval engraver known as the Master of the Amsterdam Print Room. The collection includes many other prints of which, so far as it is known, there are no other impressions. In addition to European prints by such major artists as Dürer, Callot, Tiepolo and Goya, the Print Room also has a representative collection of Japanese colour woodcuts.

While prints constitute the bulk of the collection, the highlights of the drawings and watercolours are those by Rembrandt and his school (p.146), the French eighteenth-century masters (p.146, p.147) and artists from various centres in Italy. German drawings form a smaller group, while a review of English water colourists is being built up.

In addition to the individual drawings, there is a collection of sketch books and albums, including some from the seventeenth-century family studio of Gerard ter Borch which contain over a thousand drawings.

The Print Room also houses separate sections for portraits, historical prints, topographical views, decorative prints, popular and children's prints, artists' holographs etc. The exhibition catalogues, over 70 of which have been published since 1960, and amongst which 40 refer to the Rijksmuseum's own collections, contain expert descriptions and information relating to the prints and drawings on display.

Henry VIII of England (1491–1547)
Cornelis Anthoniesz (Amsterdam *c* 1499–
Amsterdam *c* 1555)
Woodcut, hand coloured; 403 × 295 mm
(PR)

The entrance to the Print Room study room, which is also that of the Rijksmuseum Library, is situated at 1a Jan Luykenstraat. Admission is free and from 10.00 to 17.00, except for Sundays and Mondays. Visitors wishing to view extremely valuable works such as Seghers' etchings must first obtain the written permission of the Director of the Print Room.

Mlle Marcelle Lender
Henri Toulouse-Lautrec (Albi 1864–
Schloss Malromé, Gironde, 1901)
Coloured lithograph; 328 × 242 mm

(PR)

Washing the feet of Christ
Rembrandt Harmensz van Rijn (Leiden
1606–Amsterdam 1669)
Pen and brown ink; 156 × 220 mm

(PR)

Three tulips and an anemone
Jacob Marrel (Frankenthal 1614–
Frankfurt 1681)
Pencil in colour on parchment;
340 × 450 mm (PR)

Seated woman with bust
Jean-Antoine Watteau (Valenciennes
1684–Nogent-sur-Marne 1721)
Red, white and black chalk on brownish
paper; 230 × 262 mm (PR)

147

(opposite)
St Mark's Square with campanile
Antonio Canaletto (Venice 1697–Venice 1768)
Pen and brown ink, pencil in grey; 235 × 225 mm

(PR)

Gorge with cliff
Hercules Segers (Haarlem *c* 1590–Amsterdam *c* 1635)
*Etching printed in black ink on cloth prepared in yellowish-brown,
then painted with yellow and white body colour; 156 × 161 mm*

(PR)

The Dam in Amsterdam
George Hendrik Breitner (Rotterdam 1857–Amsterdam 1923)
Pencil and aquarel; 403 × 513 mm (PR)

150

Asiatic Art

Eastern art is represented in nearly every department of the Rijksmuseum: the Dutch History Department has objects deriving from Dutch ventures in the East; the Department of Sculpture and Decorative Arts has a collection of 'colonial art' (objects made in the countries of the East but commissioned by Dutch people living there) and the Print Room contains a magnificent collection of Japanese graphic art. Chinese and Japanese porcelain can be found in various parts of the museum. As an important article of trade this was part of Dutch history; from the seventeenth century onwards it was a common item in many Dutch households, but it also constituted the main influence on the development of Dutch and European ceramics and has long been prized as applied art.

The Department of Asiatic Art is situated at the back of the museum and has its own entrance. It concentrates, as its name implies, on works from Asiatic countries which can be considered as representative of important movements or styles in art. Thus the Department possesses sculpture, painting and applied art from Eastern Asia (China, Japan, Korea), with slightly less material from Southern Asia (India, Pakistan, Bangladesh, Nepal and Sri Lanka) and South-east Asia (Burma, Cambodia, Thailand, Vietnam and Indonesia). Some of the most striking items are a fine collection of Chinese porcelain (p.152, p.156); a very beautiful Chinese wood and polychrome statue of a seated Avalokiteshvara (Kuan Yin) of the twelfth century (p.150); a twelve-leaved album painted by the eccentric Kao Ch'i–pei (1662?–1731?) with his fingers and nails (p.157); a fourteenth-century Korean chest for Buddhist manuscripts (one of the very few surviving examples of wood inlaid with mother-of-pearl and metal thread from such an early period); an important collection of Japanese ceramics, mainly objects used in the tea ceremony, with some items dating from the end of the sixteenth century (p.153); a number of magnificent pieces of Japanese lacquer work dating from the sixteenth to the twentieth centuries, and a pair of early seventeenth-century room screens showing the Portuguese in the harbour of Nagasaki (p.153).

Indonesia is represented by a fine collection of stone and metal sculptures dating mainly from the middle Javanese period (c 7th–10th century). A highly unusual bronze statue of a standing Buddha (p.155), made in Southern India or Ceylon and found in East Java, provides evidence of the centuries-old movement of culture from India to South-east Asia, while the famous figure of Shiva, Lord of the Dance (p.155), is a marvellous example of the high standard of bronze casting under the Cola dynasty.

The Association of Friends of Asiatic Art deserves mention in this context: its endeavours to increase public awareness and appreciation of Asiatic art led to the setting up of the Department, and many of the items on display come from its collection.

Avalokiteshvara (Kuan Yin)
China, 12th century
Wood with polychrome; H. 107 cm   (CAA)

151

(top)
Ceremonial wine vessel (yü)
China, end Shang period, Anyang style,
12th–11th century BC
Bronze; H. 12 cm   (CAA)

Large jar
China, 1st half 15th century
Porcelain with blue under-glaze;
H. 45 cm   (CAA)

**Casing for a bamboo pillar in the
form of a celestial nymph
surrounded by clouds**
Indonesia, East Javanese period,
Mojopahit, 14th century
Terracotta; H. 35 cm   (CAA)

**Pair of Namban room screens
showing a Portuguese ship arriving
in Nagasaki harbour**
Japan, early 17th century
*Ink, colours and gold on paper; H. 169 cm,
W. 363 cm*   (CAA)

Tea bowl
Japan, end 16th century
*Raku ware with gold lacquer repair;
H. 7.5 cm, Diam. 13.8 cm*   (CAA)

Shiva Guru
Indonesia, Middle Javanese period (*c* 7th–
10th century)
Volcanic stone; H. 100 cm   (CAA)

Head of a Buddha
Cambodia, Vat Rom Lok style, end 7th
century
Stone; H. 26 cm   (CAA)

Shiva, Lord of the Dance
India, Cola Dynasty, 12th century
Bronze; H. 154 cm   (CAA)

Pot with four ears
Vietnam, 15th century
Earthenware with blue under-glaze;
H. 30 cm   (CAA)

Standing Buddha
South India or Sri Lanka, late Amaravati
style, 8th century
Bronze; H. 42 cm
Found in eastern Java.   (CAA)

Landscape painting
China, by Kao Ch'i-p'ei (1662–1731?)
Ink and colours on paper; 27×33 cm

(CAA)

(opposite)
Series of twelve cups
China, K'ang Hsi (1662–1722)
Porcelain with blue under-glaze and enamels; H. 4.7 cm, D. 6.5 cm
Each cup is decorated with a plant or flower, together with a poem
treating one of the twelve months. (CAA)

Avalokiteshvara
Nepal, 14th century
Gilded bronze; H. 23.2 cm (CAA)

Jar
Korea, 12th–13th century
*Earthenware with Celadon glaze and inlay, and gold lacquer repair;
H. 34 cm* (CAA)

Studieverzamelingen
Collections d'étude
Study Collections
Studiensammlungen

Aziatische kunst
Art Asiatique
Asiatic Art
Asiatische Kunst

Studieverzamelingen
Collections d'étude
Study Collections
Studiensammlungen

Beeldhouwkunst & Kunstnijverheid
Sculpture & Arts Décoratifs
Sculpture & Applied Art
Plastik & Kunstgewerbe

Nederlandse Geschiedenis
Histoire des Pays-Bas
Dutch History
Niederländische Geschichte

Islamitische kunst
Art Islamique
Islamic Art
Islamitische Kunst

Beeldhouwkunst & Kunstnijverheid
Sculpture & Arts Décoratifs
Sculpture & Applied Art
Plastik & Kunstgewerbe

Rijksprentenkabinet
Cabinet des Estampes
Print Room
Kupferstichkabinett

Schilderkunst 18de en 19de eeuw
Peinture 18ème et 19ème siècles
Paintings 18th and 19th century
Malerei 18. und 19. Jht.

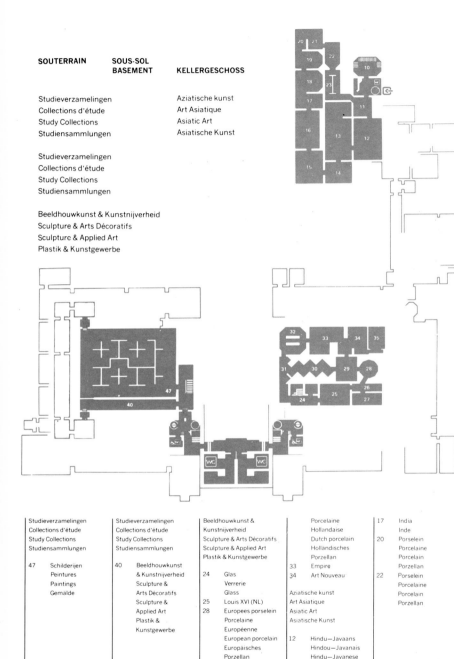

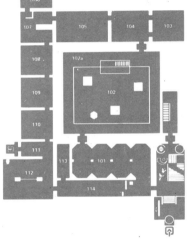

Studieverzamelingen	Studieverzamelingen	Beeldhouwkunst &	Porcelaine	17 India
Collections d'étude	Collections d'étude	Kunstnijverheid	Hollandaise	Inde
Study Collections	Study Collections	Sculpture & Arts Décoratifs	Dutch porcelain	20 Porselein
Studiensammlungen	Studiensammlungen	Sculpture & Applied Art	Hollandisches	Porcelaine
		Plastik & Kunstgewerbe	Porzellan	Porcelain
47 Schilderijen	40 Beeldhouwkunst		33 Empire	Porzellan
Peintures	& Kunstnijverheid	24 Glas	34 Art Nouveau	22 Porselein
Paintings	Sculpture &	Verrerie		Porcelaine
Gemälde	Arts Décoratifs	Glass	Aziatische kunst	Porcelain
	Sculpture &	25 Louis XVI (NL)	Art Asiatique	Porzellan
	Applied Art	28 Europees porselein	Asiatic Art	
	Plastik &	Porcelaine	Asiatische Kunst	
	Kunstgewerbe	Européenne		
		European porcelain	12 Hindu—Javaans	
		Europäisches	Hindou—Javanais	
		Porzellan	Hindu—Javanese	
		29 Louis XVI (NL)	Hindu—Javanisch	
		30 Kostuums	13 Japan	
		Costumes	Japon	
		Kostume	14 Japan	
		31 Kant	Japon	
		Dentelle	Japan	
		Lace	15 China	
		Spitzen	Chine	
		32 Hollands porselein	16 China	
			Chine	

Nederlandse Geschiedenis	Harnassen, wapens	Chaire
Histoire des Pays-Bas	Armures, armes	Pulpit
Dutch History	Armour	Kanzel
Niederländische Geschichte	Harnische, Waffen	114 Uurwerk
	102a Dagelijks leven	Horloge
101 Elisabethsvloed	La vie quotidienne	Clock
Inondation de la	Everyday life	Pendeluhr
Ste. Elisabeth	Alltagsleben	
Elizabeth's flood	Penningen	
Elisabeth-Flut	Médailles	Beeldhouwkunst &
102 17de eeuw	Medals	Kunstnijverheid
17ème siècle	Denkmünzen	Sculpture & Arts Décoratifs
17th century	103 Royal Charles,	Sculpture & Applied Art
17. Jht.	Chatham	Plastik & Kunstgewerbe
V.O.C.	104 Admiraals	162 Poppenhuizen
Comp. des Indes	Amiraux	Maisons de
East India Company	Admirals	Dolls' Houses
Ostindische	Admiräle	Puppenhäuser
Kompagnie	107 Verre Oosten	163 Beeldhouwkunst
Nova Zembla	Extrême-Orient	Sculpture
Novaja Semlja	Far East	Plastik
Scheepsmodellen	Ferner Osten	166 Kant
Maquettes de bateaux	Deshima	Dentelle
Ship Models	110 Waterloo, Pieneman	Lace
Schiffsmodelle	112 Preekstoel	Spitzen

EERSTE VERDIEPING   **PREMIER ÉTAGE**
FIRST FLOOR   **ERSTER STOCK**

Schilderkunst 15de—17de eeuw
Peinture 15ème—17ème siècle
Paintings 15th—17th century
Malerei 15.—17. Jht.

Beeldhouwkunst & Kunstnijverheid
Sculpture & Arts Décoratifs
Sculpture & Applied Art
Plastik & Kunstgewerbe

Tijdelijke tentoonstellingen
Expositions temporaires
Temporary exhibitions
Sonderausstellungen

Ingang museum / Entrée du musée / Museum Entrance / Museumeingang

Lift / Ascenseur / Lift / Elevator / Aufzug

Informatie / Information

Filmzaal / Films / Film Theatre / Filmsaal

Educatieve Dienst / Service Educatif / Education Department / Padagogischer Dienst

Reproduktie- en catalogusverkoop / Livres et Reproductions / Books and Reproductions / Bücher und Reproduktionen

Bibliotheek / Bibliothèque / Library / Bibliothek

WC voor invaliden / WC pour invalides / WC for handicapped / Invalidentoilette

Telefoon / Téléphone / Telephone / Telefon

Postzegels / Timbres / Stamps / Briefmarken

Rookkamer / Fumoir / Smoking Room / Rauchzimmer

Restaurant

Schilderkunst
18de en 19de eeuw
Peinture
18ème et 19ème siècles
Paintings
18th and 19th century
Malerei 18. und 19. Jht.

142   18de—19de eeuw
    18ème—19ème siècle
    18th—19th century
    18.—19. Jht.
143   19de eeuw
    19ème siècle
    19th century
    19. Jht.
147   Haagse School
    Ecole de la Haye
    The Hague School
    Haager Schule
148   — id.
149   Amsterdamse School
    Ecole d'Amsterdam
    Amsterdam School
    Amsterdamer Schule

Islamitische kunst
Art Islamique
Islamic Art
Islamitische Kunst

138   Islamitische Kunst
    Art Islamique
    Islamic Art
    Islamitische Kunst
141   Chinees porselein
    Porcelaine de Chine
    Chinese porcelain
    Chinesisches
    Porzellan

Rijksprentenkabinet
Cabinet des Estampes
Print Room
Kupferstichkabinett

128   Tentoonstellingen
    Expositions
    Exhibitions
    Ausstellungen
129 — 133 — id.

Schilderkunst
15de—17de eeuw
Peintures 15ème—17ème siècle
Paintings 15th—17th century
Malerei 15.—17. Jht.

201   15de eeuw
    15ème siècle
    15th century
    15. Jht.
202   — id.
203   — id.
204   16de eeuw
    16ème siècle
    16th century
    16. Jht.
205 — 209 — id.
211   Frans Hals
211a   — id.
214a   Van Goyen
214   Ruisdael
215   Van der Helst
216   Jan Steen
217   Italianisanten
    Italianisants

220   Rembrandt
221   — id.
221a   Vermeer
222a   — id.
222   Rembrandtschool
    Ecole de Rembrandt
    Rembrandt School
    Rembrandt Schule
224   NACHTWACHT
    RONDE DE NUIT
    NIGHTWATCH
    NACHTWACHE
229 — 236   Buitenlandse scholen
    Ecoles étrangères
    Foreign Schools
    Ausländische Schulen
229   Italië
    Italy
    Italien
230 — 232 — id.
233   Spanje
    Espagne

Italianizers
Spain
Spanien
234   Frankrijk
    France
    Frankreich
235   Vlaanderen
    Flandre
    Flanders
    Flandern
236   Italië
    Italy
    Italien

Beeldhouwkunst & Kunstnijverheid
Sculpture & Arts Décoratifs
Sculpture & Applied Art
Plastik & Kunstgewerbe

238   Middeleeuwen
    Moyen Age
    Middle Ages
    Mittelalter
239 — 242 — id.
248   Italië
    Italy
    Italien
250   Renaissance
251a   Schatkamer
    Trésors
    Treasure Room
    Schatzkammer
253   Glas. Zilver
    Verrerie, Argenterie
    Glass. Silver
    Glas. Silber
253a   Koloniale kunst
    Art Colonial

Kolonialkunst
254   Lutma, Vianen
255   Delfts aardewerk
    Faience de Delft
    Delft
    Delfter Fayence
256 — 257 — id.
258   Quellinus. Verhulst
    Beeldhouwkunst
    Sculpture
    Plastik

159

Index

Page references are to illustration pages